MW01078944

From A
to Eames

From A to Eames

A Visual Guide to Mid-Century Modern Design

Lauren Whybrow *with illustrations by* Tom Jay

Smith Street Books

Contents

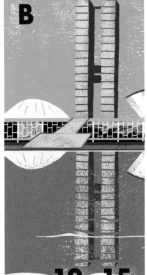

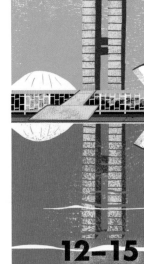

L 52–55

M 56–59

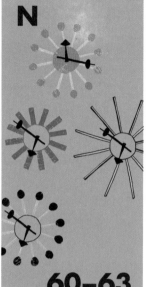

N 60–63

O 64–67

P 68–71

Q 72–75

R 76–79

S 80–83

T 84–87

U 88–91

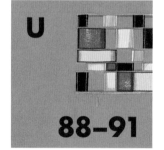

V 92–95

W 96–99

X 100–101

Y 102–105

Z 106–109

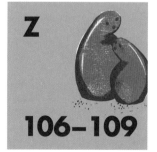

Timeline 110

Introduction

When Charles and Ray Eames released their fibreglass moulded plastic chair in 1950, it was the first single-shell plastic chair to be mass-produced, and it changed the way that people sat.

This was the first of many firsts for the Eameses, whose voracious appetite for making products better extended across chairs, tables, ads, books, homes.

They weren't alone in their drive for better design. The architects, industrial and interior designers, and even salespeople behind mid-century modern design were pioneering in their attempts to create a brighter future through better design. This brighter future wasn't just for the elite few, but for the many, as finally technology existed to mass-produce objects on a scale that made designer furniture, well, more affordable.

That's what mid-century modern was all about: creating good designs that functioned well, looked great and were able to be mass-produced. The designers in this book – often separated by years and countries – were unified in their creativity, their inventiveness and their push to use new materials and new techniques, to reconsider everything from how people sit to how they use a kitchen. But these crazy ideas weren't possible simply due to material advances, but due to a consumer drive for material goods.

Though mid-century modern made its first, tentative strides towards becoming a design movement in the 1920s (although the movement was only named retrospectively), it didn't hit its stride until the end of World War II. By the 1950s, with the end of rationing and when people, materials and disposable cash were suddenly in supply again, the future looked brighter than a Hollywood star's smile.

For the first time, people could have what stars like Frank Sinatra (a famous fan of mid-century modern) had ... as long as they could afford the deliberately reasonable prices. That's because mid-century modern wasn't just about being egalitarian. It was about consumerism; good design had become a readily accessible commodity, and a marker of lifestyle.

But the people featured in this book didn't make items to just look good or to make cash. They designed items, homes and cities to function, to be tactile, to improve lives. It was about designing a kettle that wouldn't leak; a spoon that would reach into a jar and get the last of the sauce; an electric light that was soft, not harsh (way better for photos); a well-designed home that could be replicated and available to more people, an idea expanded on a huge scale through the modern cities planned by leading modernist architects around the world.

Mid-century modern design changed the way you sit, eat and live. Even though you might not be able to afford the original pieces featured in this book – ironically, they are now expensive collectors' items – you probably use a few items every day that were influenced by mid-century modern designers and products, from your cutlery to the seats around your dining-room table. More than just making our homes (and cafes and offices) look better, mid-century modern's lasting impact was that design could make lives better, including making good design available to pretty much everyone.

So sit down in a chair – maybe an Eames lounge, if there's one handy – and discover the people and products that, perhaps more than any other era, have shaped the look of our world today.

A is for
Aalto

If you've seen an IKEA plywood stool, then you've seen a replica of an Alvar Aalto design – his famous Stool 60. This design is so common now that it's hard to believe it was once revolutionary, but the technique that he used to curve the three birch legs and attach them to the seat was pioneering, as was the stool's simple and pared-back look.

Alvar Aalto was more than just the man behind the world's most famous stool. As an architect, industrial designer and thinker, he came to represent the burgeoning of Finnish modernist design.

He didn't do this alone. Most of his furniture, and early houses and public buildings, were designed in collaboration with his first wife, Aino Aalto, although her name is often dropped from the credits. Alvar set up his own studio in 1923, which Aino joined in 1924. They married the same year. While Aino and Alvar's homes and designs are functional, an essential trait for anything modernist, they are also decorative and warm, using materials native to Finland and organic shapes that reflect nature.

All of the projects that people gush over, like the seminal Paimio Sanatorium, a treatment centre for people with tuberculosis that's considered one of the most important modernist buildings of the 20th century, were a collaboration between the two designers. At Paimio, everything from the initial site plans down to the sinks in the patients' bedrooms were created by the pair.

This prolific couple designed everything from hospitals, houses, chairs, lamps, trolleys, glassware and building interiors. It's impossible, now, to work out exactly what they designed together or separately: while Alvar led the architecture arm of his studio, Aino came up with many of the interiors for these buildings, and was the creative director of their furniture company, Artek.

After Aino's death in 1949, Alvar continued designing, working on large and still lasting public buildings, including the Finland House of Culture and Jyväskylä University.

A is also for

Antelope chair by Ernest Race

Considered quite racy when it was released, the Antelope chair by Ernest Race was a leap forward in modern furniture design. This thoroughly British chair was designed for the outdoor spaces of 1951's Festival of Britain, which was meant to excite British people about the future of being, well, British. The chair was both functional, built using leftover armaments material from World War II, and playful, with a simple steel frame and curved wooden seat that looked like the sketched outline of a traditional armchair.

Anni Albers

Anni Albers' textiles were works of art. She was the most influential textile artist of the 20th century, and the first to receive a solo show at the Museum of Modern Art (MoMA) in New York. Her work was both traditional and experimental: it was informed by the weaving techniques of Central and South America, but she also played around with patterns and materials, including plastic and wire.

Yet she almost didn't become a weaver.

Born in 1899 in Berlin, she applied to Germany's pioneering Bauhaus school to study glasswork or painting. But those classes weren't open to women, so she trained in a discipline that was open to her — weaving. It was there she discovered the possibilities of a single line of thread. Her graduation piece was a wall-hanging for an auditorium: a piece of decorative art, but one with a practical function, made of cotton woven with cellophane to absorb more sound.

Anni was Head of Weaving when Bauhaus shut under pressure from the new Nazi government in 1933. She moved to America with her husband, Josef. Both initially taught at the experimental Black Mountain College in North Carolina.

After Anni's solo show at MoMA in 1949, Florence Knoll (p.48) asked Anni to produce textiles for furniture company Knoll, that could be replicated and sold en-masse as upholstery or wall tapestries; one of the designs that Anni produced was the bestselling Eclat weave.

American Modern

For Americans in the late 1930s, embracing a new style of living meant packing away the ornate and ornamental good china and embracing the casual, shapely and multi-coloured tableware of Russel Wright's American Modern, illustrated below. This simple tableware might not look particularly groundbreaking now, but when it was released in 1939, American Modern represented a new American style of living – and at a price point millions could afford. The range also sold millions of pieces between 1939 and 1959, making it the bestselling tableware of all time.

Together with his wife, Mary, who was a bit of a marketing genius, Russel became the figurehead for this new casual American lifestyle. Their book, *Guide to Easier Living*, was a blueprint on how to live a modern life, advocating for open-plan homes full of good design – and a set of American Modern tableware, of course.

B is for

Brasília

Brazil's capital city, Brasília, was born of a utopian vision and made as a big democratic statement, as well as being part of President Juscelino Kubitschek's plan to revitalise Brazil's interior by moving the capital city from Rio de Janeiro to a new inland site. When Brasília was completed in 1960, it looked like the city of the future: it was orderly, uniform and concrete, designed to the modernist ideals of the Functional City.

Famous Brazilian architect Oscar Niemeyer and urban planner Lúcio Costa designed Brasília with input from landscape designer Roberto Burle Marx. From above, it looked like a plane, perhaps propelling its citizens toward a bright and prosperous future. The main street, aptly named Eixo Monumental, runs through the city like a fuselage. The residential blocks – each one meant to operate as a mini city – spread out from Eixo Monumental like wings.

Eixo Monumental was also home to the city's largest and most important buildings, including Niemeyer's grand government buildings, formed of concrete geometric shapes that have more in common with the work of an avant-garde ceramicist than your regular public service buildings. The most well-known of these buildings is the National Congress – a long, low glass building notable for the dome and bowl perched on opposite ends of the roof, with two 27-storey office buildings, which housed the practical operations of government, rising from the middle.

Despite its utopian aspirations, many people think Brasília is more dystopian: overly planned and cold. It's all a matter of perspective, but from above the vision for this UNESCO World Heritage Site still looks big and bold.

B is also for

Lina Bo Bardi

Lina Bo Bardi was the architect responsible for some of the most striking buildings in her adopted home city of São Paulo in Brazil. There's MASP, a glass art gallery raised on red pillars to form a public plaza underneath; the SESC Pompéia, an old factory that she converted into a concrete community centre, which rises into the sky; and her own home, Glass House, an almost transparent building on stilts that appears to float in remnant rainforest, just like it floats on the page below. She believed in the potential of architecture to improve life, to encourage community, and she worked in close collaboration with the people who would use her buildings – most often the people of São Paulo.

Born in Italy in 1917, Lina Bo Bardi moved to Brazil with her husband in 1946 (some say on a whim, others say her Communist leanings were causing trouble in Italy's post-war political environment). She'd been an established modernist architect and thinker in Italy, working with the likes of Gio Ponti (p.71) and Carlo Pagani. But when Bo Bardi moved, she adapted her work to the Brazilian vernacular; while she still worked with modernist materials like steel, glass and concrete, she also introduced traditional Brazilian materials like mud and straw.

This might make her sound Establishment. She wasn't. In her final speech, given in 1991, she proclaimed herself a Stalinist and an anti-feminist. Yet even though her speech and ideas might have been alienating, her buildings are anything but: welcoming spaces for all parts of the community to enjoy.

Luis Barragán

Luis Barragán created a world of colour and surprises, of light and shadow. His homes inspire joy, and make you want to move in (if only). It's no wonder that he was Mexico's most famous architect.

Born in 1902, the independently wealthy Barragán travelled around Europe in the 1920s, where he saw modernist buildings and met modernist architects, including Le Corbusier (p.52). Inspired, he returned home to Mexico and started designing buildings, mainly homes, that took the ideas of European modernism and made them local.

Barragán's buildings are distinctive — while many present a blank wall to the street, the interiors are magic realms of colour, splashed with bright yellows, pinks and blues: like a modest entrance hallway made remarkable by yellow walls, leading down a rabbit hole into a pink double-height room.

Don't make the mistake of thinking this use of colour was just superficial. Barragán's colours often reflected the Mexican climate and influenced how people would use a space, such as the cool blue room with a cool pool deep inside his Casa Gilardi, the only light coming from a skylight. It's a tranquil retreat from the heat.

When you step into one of his homes, you step into a world of unexpected delight — just the way he wanted it.

C is for

Case Study Houses

It was 1945 in America and World War II had just been won. Suddenly, resources that had been poured into the war effort – people, money and materials – were available again. At the same time America, particularly Los Angeles, was booming; it needed more homes, and it needed them fast. The country was primed and ready to leave the privations of war in the past and go warp-speed into the bright new future of peace, cooperation and consumerism. But what would that look like?

John Entenza, the pioneering editor and owner of *Arts & Architecture* magazine, wasn't about to let that future decide itself without some prodding towards good design. He came up with the Case Study Houses Program, to be run through the magazine, inspired by the earlier modernist project of Weissenhof Estate in Stuttgart. For his program, Entenza commissioned the best modernist architects around – or at least in California – to design modern houses using modern materials and techniques. These houses had to be replicable, their fabric affordable and prefabricated. Once completed, the houses would be open to the public for a short time, so people could see these glamorous calling cards of mid-century modern architecture and design for themselves, and then want to build their own.

Entenza recruited architects like Raphael Soriano (p.83), Charles Eames (later joined by his partner and wife, Ray, p.24), Eero Saarinen, Craig Ellwood (p.26) and Richard Neutra (p.62) to join the program. There were only meant to be eight houses, to be built on a block of land Entenza owned in Pacific Palisades, but 36 ended up being designed and 24 were built, with later architects invited to join the program bringing their own clients and own land.

Ultimately, none of the homes were replicated. But while the architects involved in the Case Study Houses Program didn't design and build the future of California, they did inspire its aesthetic. It was up to developers like Joseph Eichler (p.27) to take these ideas and make them mass-producible by building mid-century modern housing estates.

A number of Case Study Houses have been demolished or renovated beyond recognition, but a few shining examples remain. The most famous is Stahl House (p.80), closely followed by Eames House, illustrated top right – a two-storey box made of glass and Mondrian-esque panels, which Charles and Ray Eames constructed next to Entenza House, as seen top middle on right, in Pacific Palisades. The houses in this program, more than any others, represent this idealistic time, when the future was just waiting to be built.

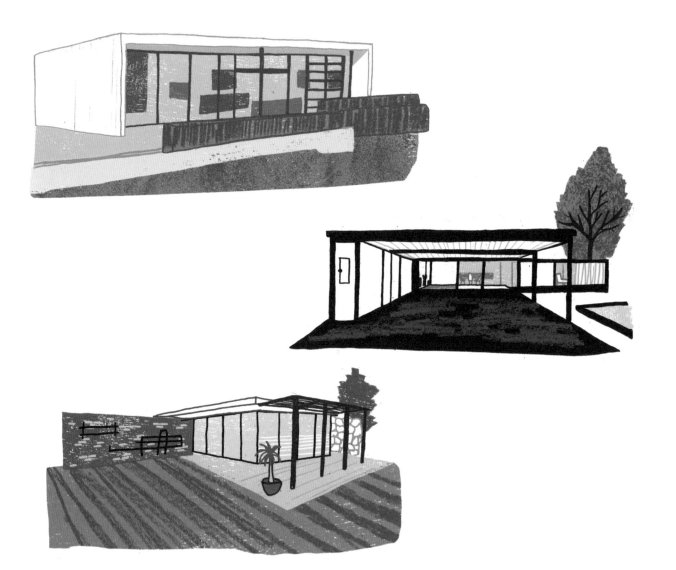

C is also for

Chandigarh

The city of Chandigarh in India, often attributed solely to Le Corbusier (p.52), was actually a collaboration between a number of architects. British architect Dame Jane Drew (p.23) and her husband and partner, Maxwell Fry, were approached by Jawaharlal Nehru, then Prime Minister of India, to design a new capital city for Punjab. This city would represent the ideals of a new India and a new age. Drew, busy with the Festival of Britain, suggested inviting Le Corbusier to join the endeavour. Naturally, Le Corbusier came up with the master plan and main buildings, based on his well-established theory of the Functional City.

He planned it as a garden city in a grid; ordered, clean and very green, with plaza after plaza forming public spaces around the grand concrete government buildings, which look like brutalist castles.

Drew and Fry were notable for spending time in the cities they planned, understanding the climate and how people lived. This was not how Le Corbusier approached Chandigarh, which was less influenced by how people lived than how he thought they *should* live — for instance, in concrete buildings, even though concrete can blister in subtropical heat.

After completing the plan, Le Corbusier mainly left Drew, Fry and Le Corbusier's partner, Pierre Jeanneret, to stay in the city and complete the practicalities. But for all that, Chandigarh, one of India's most affluent and liveable cities, is a success — a big idea that worked.

Cap Moderne

Cap Moderne is a small modernist enclave amid the bikinis, billionaires and brash opulence of the Côte d'Azur in the south of France. This area, which is now a designated architectural attraction, is home to the E-1027 summer house designed by Irish architect and designer Eileen Gray (p.32), and Le Corbusier's holiday *cabanon* and his holiday shacks. While the heritage-listed *cabanon* is worth a look, it's E-1027 that demands your attention: a home of beauty in both design and location, and simply one of the most aesthetically pleasing buildings in the world.

As you stare at the white lines of Gray's raised rectangular house, its easy-breezy interior with open spaces — and enough secret ones to be intriguing — you'd think that life here has been like something from a dream, where the sun always shines at cocktail hour. But this home has seen break-ups, vandalism (from Le Corbusier himself, no less) and murder. Yet it's still as beautiful as ever; one of the earliest examples of a modernist house that was actually liveable.

Castiglioni

While 'C' stands for Castiglioni, it could just as well stand for 'curious'. Achille Castiglioni was an Italian industrial designer who was endlessly curious; he approached his work with warmth and playfulness. His objects were not designed to sit on pedestals, but to be touched, used, sat on and moved around.

After graduating from the Polytechnic University of Milan in 1944, Achille worked with his brothers, Livio (who left the firm in 1952) and Pier Giacomo (who worked with Achille until Pier's death in 1968).

Achille's most famous design is the Arco lamp, a floor lamp with a long metal arm curving up from a marble base, ending with a punctuation mark of a silver mushroom shade, as illuminated above. This design is classic, almost restrained – especially compared to Castiglioni's Mezzadro stool, which has a tractor seat; or the Sleek plastic spoon, designed to help you get every last bit of food from a jar. There seemed to be no end to his talent, which didn't stop at industrial design, but also encompassed architecture and teaching.

D is for

Day

Forget where you are for a second and imagine yourself back to the 1950s, seeing Lucienne Day's abstract Calyx fabric or Robin Day's polypropylene chairs for the first time. They had new patterns, new materials, new shapes — it was modern and thrilling.

Lucienne and Robin Day were Britain's answer to the Eameses (p.24), a design couple for the modern age who were thrifty, inventive and commercially minded, with a house on Cheyne Walk in Chelsea next to Bianca and Mick Jagger. They met at the Royal College of Art in 1940 — Lucienne was studying textiles and Robin, furniture design — and married in 1942.

It wasn't all riches and the Rolling Stones straight away. Throughout World War II, both spent time teaching to supplement their design work. But by 1951, the Days and the British public were ready for something different. The Clem Atlee Labour government decided that British citizens didn't need to stay calm anymore; it was time to look forward to the future. The Festival of Britain was meant to spark that excitement. Robin was invited to make all of the seating for the new Festival Hall, as well as design two rooms that would feature his furnishings, set off by Lucienne's textiles.

For one of these rooms, Lucienne designed the Calyx fabric. It was wildly different to any other pattern on the market, an abstract representation of plants in lines and geometric shapes. Lucienne wanted this fabric to be affordable, so it could liven up the homes of ordinary people looking for some colour and modern taste in their homes. She convinced furniture store Heal's to support it, although they offered her a low fee because they expected it would be a commercial failure. Instead the fabric was an immediate bestseller.

Conversely, after his success at the Festival of Britain creating chairs that sparked the imagination, Robin started making chairs that are now seen as decidedly utilitarian, including possibly the most successful chair in the world, the cheap and stackable polypropylene moulded chair (you've probably sat on one at your local school and community hall).

After these early successes, Lucienne and Robin continued designing prolifically, spending the rest of their careers working across from each other in their home studio.

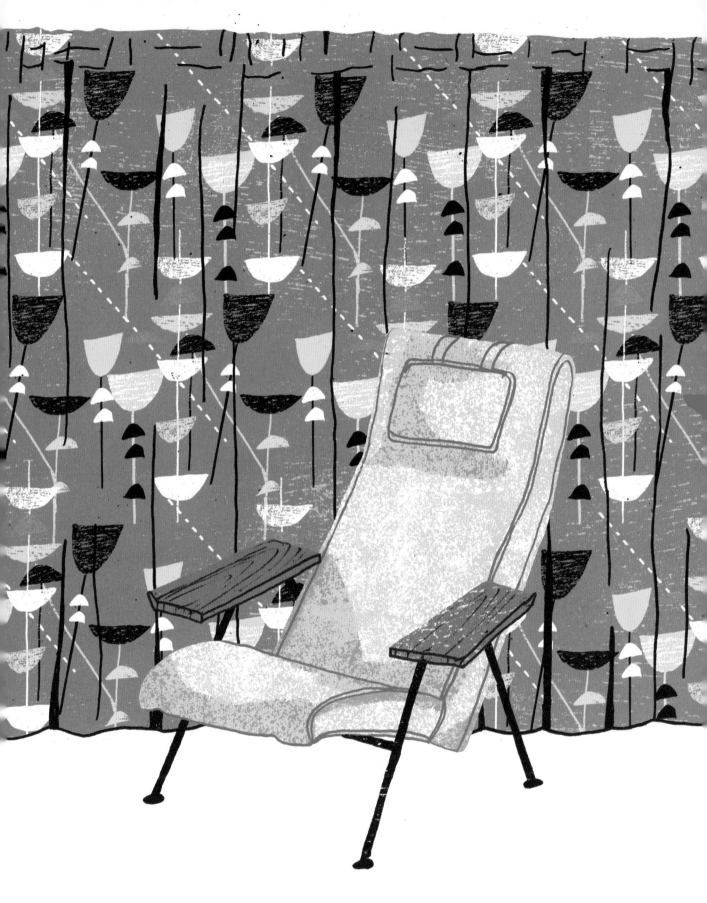

D is also for

Diamond chair

When furniture company Knoll (p.48) released Harry Bertoia's Diamond chair in 1952, the chair was that rarity – a true original. Its wide diamond-shaped body was formed by a grid of metal rods; it was halfway between a sculpture and a chair, which you can marvel at in the illustration below.

Bertoia was born in Italy in 1915 and moved to Detroit when he was 15. He won a scholarship to Cranbrook Academy of Art, where he met Florence Knoll, who, along with her husband, would later turn Knoll into a powerhouse of mid-century modern design. Bertoia started out learning painting, but soon changed to metalwork. After graduating, he taught at Cranbrook, then moved to Los Angeles to work with the Eameses. This is no place for gossip, but he didn't love working for them, and in 1950 Knoll invited him to move to Pennsylvania and design a metal chair for her.

The Diamond chair was the result of two years of experimentation. Upon release, it was wildly successful and is still in production today.

Dame Jane Drew

Dame Jane Drew was a mentor, a friend, and an indomitable enthusiast for architecture and well-designed places. She was a modernist who considered how people would use a space and how a building would fit within a local environment.

Born in England in 1911, Drew looked for work after graduating from architecture school in the 1930s, but there was no work in traditional studios – at least, not for a woman. So she set up her own.

Being female in a male-dominated industry gave Drew a different perspective. While designers like Le Corbusier (p.52) and Finn Juhl (p.47) measured their own bodies and designed furniture around the golden ratio of a man, Drew, similarly to Charlotte Perriand (p.88), considered how women use spaces within the home. When invited by the Gas Board to design the height of a new standard oven, she did something truly revolutionary – she designed the height for the average woman, not a man.

Her larger projects – including being part of the team that designed and built Chandigarh in India (p.18), buildings for the University of Ibadan in Nigeria and the Institute for Contemporary Art in London – are similarly thoughtfully well-considered and sympathetic to the people who would use the buildings, as well as being striking examples of modernist architecture.

E is for

Eames

If you think about America after World War II, you might imagine a wildly optimistic place – high on victory, the future and the caffeine from a trillion newly opened coffee shops. Anything and everything seemed possible. No one epitomised this more than Charles and Ray Eames, two designers whose works were crazy feats of imagination made real.

Charles was an architect; Ray was an artist. Charles has, erroneously, been given most of the credit; Ray had the creative eye that made the Eames name a famous brand. Although they did some work separately, Charles and Ray Eames did their best work together.

They met at Cranbrook Academy of Art, one of America's incubators of modernist thought. He was married, but got a divorce, and together the couple moved to Los Angeles in the 1940s. They initially worked for the war effort in a plywood factory, before setting up their own office, which thrived in the post-war era.

Their creativity and collaboration resulted in the extensive output of the Eames Office, the creative studio where they produced their wide body of work with the help of their many staff. Forget about Andy Warhol's Factory – the Eames Office was where the most exciting work in the country was happening: everything from films for government and ads for Herman Miller, to art, homes, offices, tables and, of course, their famous chairs.

There's an undeniable sense of fun in the Eameses' work; they took pleasure seriously, both in their work and their lives. It's the joy of a tiny bird peeking through the legs of Eames chairs in an ad the Eames Office designed for Herman Miller; it's the sound sculpture the Eameses invited visitors to their house to play.

Of course, Charles and Ray are now most famous for their chairs. The Eameses pioneered a new way of curving plywood, which allowed them to design a chair to closely contour to the human form, as seen in their 1946 Plywood chair. But Charles was driven by a long-held desire to make a single-shell chair without a join in sight. So they continued experimenting with materials including steel and plastic until they made the Eames Plastic chair, the first single-shell chair to enter the market and the first plastic chair to be mass-produced – and now one of the most copied chairs in the world. Their other most famous chair, the Eames lounge, was initially designed for their friend Billy Wilder (yes, *that* Billy Wilder) as a present, before it achieved wide commercial success through manufacturer Herman Miller.

There's a moment in one of the Eames Office's later films, *The Power of Ten*, where a camera zooms out at the power of 10 until you see the whole universe in front of you. You couldn't find a more apt analogy for the endless curiosity of the Eameses if you tried.

E is also for

Ercol

Ercol is a furniture company established in the United Kingdom in 1920 by Italian immigrant Lucien Ercolani; but it wasn't until the British government tasked Ercol with creating a mass-produced modern version of the Windsor chair as part of the Utility Furniture Scheme that Ercol bounced to the forefront of mid-century modern design. The defining feature of the Utility Furniture Scheme was that resources, particularly wood, had to be used efficiently. Ercol pioneered a new way of steaming wood, which meant they could use elm, an historically difficult and unpliable material. After the war, Ercol's modern Windsor chair formed the basis of the company's new Originals line, and they showcased this line at the Britain Can Make It festival in 1946, and again at the Festival of Britain in 1951.

Craig Ellwood

Craig Ellwood was the James Bond of mid-century modern design — his life was a bunch of lies, cocktails, women, good design, good looks and excellent branding. Born Johnnie Burke in 1922, he opened a building company with his brother and two friends after World War II, which they called Craig Ellwood. When that went bust, Johnnie legally changed his name to Craig Ellwood, and found work in a construction firm. Here he met John Entenza, editor of *Arts & Architecture* magazine and founder of the Case Study Houses Program (p.16), and the man who would end up championing Ellwood's work as an architect.

Ellwood wasn't a trained architect; he didn't even complete his study as a structural engineer. Yet there was no doubt he was naturally gifted, and he designed some of the most famous examples of mid-century modern architecture in Los Angeles, including three homes for the Case Study Houses Program; his Case Study House 16 is now on the National Register of Historic Places Program. But when we say 'designed', we mean came up with the initial grand idea. He left the details, including plans, to the accredited architects working in his office. Ellwood spent the twilight years of his life living with his fourth wife in Italy. Which is just how we imagine James Bond would go out, actually.

Joseph Eichler

It's not often we can portray a housing developer as a good guy. Enter Joseph Eichler, the developer most responsible for bringing mid-century modern homes to the mass market. A successful dairy salesman, Eichler decided to enter the real estate game in California by building and selling modern homes in modern estates. He hired some of the biggest and best architects in Californian modernism, including A. Quincy Jones (p.72) and Raphael Soriano (p.83), to help him accomplish this. From 1949 to 1966, Eichler built over 11,000 homes and changed the look of California.

Eichler took the ideals of mid-century modern design and mass-produced them through his housing estates. The houses on his estates weren't uniform, but they all featured almost windowless facades, like in the illustration above, which hid open-plan living areas and big glass windows out the back that blurred the lines between the house and the backyard. To Eichler, good design really was for everyone (his estates, unlike many at the time, were not segregated), as long as you could pay his – eminently reasonable – price for it.

F is for

Farnsworth House

In the middle of a paddock in Illinois sits a house. Trees gracefully shade the building; in fact, it looks a lot like the illustration below. The house is simple, a white rectangular structure raised off the ground on short white plinths, with a patio extending from the main structure that has floating steps connecting it to another, lower platform halfway between the ground and the house.

Peek inside the house – go on, you can, the walls are entirely glass, framed within white steel columns. It's one room, wrapped around a timber core that contains functions like a kitchen, a bathroom and a closet or two. It looks more like the setting for an avant-garde performance piece or a pavilion for a tea ceremony than a holiday house.

This is Farnsworth House, completed in 1950. It's one of the most famous homes in America – albeit one that attracts bugs, is hard to heat and cool, offers no privacy, and floods on occasion. The build also went massively over budget. It's no wonder that the house's original owner, Dr Edith Farnsworth, didn't like it that much.

She'd used a modest inheritance to hire leading International Style modernist architect Ludwig Mies van der Rohe to design a modern house for her. She had wanted a home; he saw an opportunity to make an architectural statement.

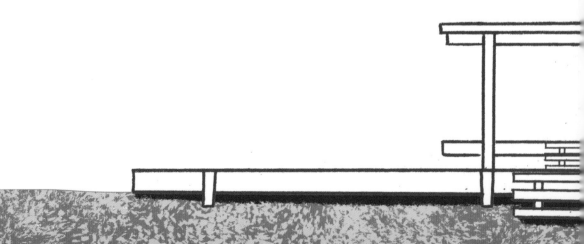

While you wouldn't be able to tell from the house's smooth, unruffled glass exterior, it was rocked by legal battles; Mies van der Rohe sued Farnsworth for unpaid construction costs and fees, and Farnsworth countersued, accusing Mies van der Rohe of fraud. Mies van der Rohe won the legal battle, leaving Farnsworth one final battlefield – the press, which delighted in throwing weighted stones at the concept of a glass house. But Mies van der Rohe eventually won over the press too, and some historians now assign Farnsworth's unhappiness with the house to a failed love affair between client and architect, regardless that little evidence exists to support this construction.

The house is now considered one of the masterpieces of American architecture ... even if it still floods on occasion.

F is also for

Kaj Franck

Finland's answer to Russel Wright (p.11) was Kaj Franck; born in 1911, he pioneered simple and attractive tableware at an affordable price. He was a designer who created items with the consumer in mind – which is why he was one of the first to design a tableware line that was sold by the individual piece, as well as pieces that could go direct from the oven or microwave to the table.

Franck designed tableware to last forever, but he also stayed current with modern consumer trends, working for a number of brands including Iittala (p. 42) and Arabia. He never wanted his name associated with his work, in case people bought plates simply because 'Kaj Franck' was on them. Instead, he wanted to design tableware that combined form and function – and would stand on its own merits. Some of his designs, including the Teema and Kartio lines, are still available and still popular.

Grant and Mary Featherston

More than any other era, mid-century modern design was defined by its partnerships – Charles and Ray Eames (p.24), Aino and Alvar Aalto (p.8), Ilmari and Annikki Tapiovaara (p.87). In Australia the couple du jour was Grant and Mary Featherston, who together came to represent the ideals of this era.

Before marrying Mary in 1965 and after serving in the armed forces in World War II, Grant established a reputation as Australia's leading chair designer. His most famous series of chairs, the Contour range, as seen in the illustration below, was released in 1951. For this line, Grant pioneered his own method of bending plywood, and the Contour R152 chair was soon found in every creative home in Australia. It also became the first chair added to the permanent collection of the National Gallery of Victoria. Mary was a prolific designer in her own right, particularly known for her work on childcare centres.

Together, Grant and Mary were even more prolific. Their first project was a chair for the Montreal Expo in 1967. Their second project was *slightly* larger, the supernova-sized task of designing the interior of the National Gallery of Victoria, where they had to create everything from the display cases to the door finishes.

Like their contemporary, Robin Boyd, they were attempting to ask and answer the question of what it meant to be Australian in the modern era through design, and came to represent a uniquely Australian approach to mid-century modern.

G is for

Gray

When Eileen Gray's Dragons chair — which she designed between 1917 and 1919 for her first major patron, Suzanne Talbot — went up for auction in 2009, it sold for £19.5 million, way over expectations. It was one of the most expensive chairs in history; not bad for a designer who many people have forgotten. Yet Eileen Gray was a pioneer — as an artist, a designer and an architect — creating notable and influential work across all the genres she worked in. It's fair to say she was somewhat of a stylistic polymath.

Gray rejected orthodoxy in her designs and in her life. She was born into an aristocratic family in Ireland in 1879, leaving to study at the Slade School of Art in London, before moving to Paris in the early 1900s. While she was in Paris she studied Japanese lacquer techniques, and started producing furniture, which she sold through her gallery. Her early work was influenced by Art Deco, just as her later work was influenced by modernism. Yet it was always, distinctly, Eileen Gray.

Her most notable work is the E-1027 on the Côte d'Azur, just around the corner from Le Corbusier's (p.52) UNESCO World Heritage—listed *cabanon*. This house has seen it all — betrayal, feuds, vandalism, murder. Yet it was originally built as a work of romance; it was Gray's first-ever architectural commission, and was designed to be a holiday home for Gray and her lover, architectural critic Jean Badovici.

The house, although reflecting modernist ideals of simplicity and harmony between built and natural environments, rejected Le Corbusier's orthodoxy that the home was a machine for living in. Gray's house was instead a living thing, where the senses could unfurl and interact with the space, which gave subtle prompts to the emotions through colour, views and textiles. She designed everything in the house, including the Bibendum chair and E-1027 table (seen in the illustration to the right), which look similar to furniture produced by Breuer, Le Corbusier and Perriand (p.88), but are more comfortable, more rotund, more interesting.

When Badovici and Gray broke up, Gray left the house and built another further down the coast. After she'd gone, Le Corbusier — originally a friend of both — visited E-1027 and painted large, sexually aggressive murals in the nude. Gray was furious.

After this, Gray stepped away from the spotlight. While her contemporaries established bigger reputations and bigger projects, she was mostly forgotten until a new generation in the 1980s rediscovered her, and her furniture was reissued.

Eileen Gray was original in style and approach, one of the first architects to blend the personal and the modern, using new materials with new style — which became markers of mid-century modern.

G is also for

Alexander Girard

Alexander Girard lived in a world full of colour, much of which he created himself throughout his prolific career. To enter Girard's 'total works of art' truly was to enter a plane of imagination and magic equal to anything created by his contemporaries like Eameses (p.24) or Nelson (p.60).

Although he trained as an architect in both London and New York, it's his work with textiles and interiors for which he's remembered, from the colourful typographic walls of his iconic La Fonda del Sol restaurant in New York, where he created everything from the menu to the pepper shakers, to the vibrant interiors of Miller House with its red conversation pit, his world of colour offset against the more austere modernist lines of the building itself as designed by Eero Saarinen.

After a stint working in a design studio in Detroit, Girard was appointed to lead the textiles division at Herman Miller, a role he held for 20 years. His designs were extensive and varied, a carnival of riotous patterns and swatches heavily influenced by the architecture and style of Florence, where he spent much of his childhood, and folk art from around the world, but particularly of the New Mexico desert.

Walter Gropius

Walter Gropius was not a mid-century modern designer, yet his influence on this period is undeniable. He founded the Bauhaus – the German university of applied and fine arts – in the wake of World War I, and it became a petri dish of talent, with Breuer, Anni (p.10) and Josef Albers, Klee, and Kandinsky, just some of the students and teachers. It was an egalitarian concept – for men, at least, since women were discouraged from joining and restricted to certain courses – that embraced art and craftspeople on an equal level, although a later focus on technology and industrial design forced some artists out.

Gropius not only built the intellectual framework of the Bauhaus, but also the physical structures of the campus in Dessau in the 1920s. These buildings – notably the three-storey glass workshop building – influenced the architecture of the 20th century, particularly as, once the Bauhaus was permanently shut in 1933, its students and teachers moved all over the world, spreading its style. Gropius himself ended up at Harvard University, where he led the School of Architecture, teaching the next generation of modernist architects.

Sir Roy Grounds

It only takes a second of looking at Sir Roy Grounds' buildings to see that he was an architect interested in geometric shapes. There's the concrete reinforced dome of the Australian Academy of Science in Canberra, his first major commission, illustrated above; the round Ship House in Mount Eliza; and the rectangular National Gallery of Victoria, the diamond Arts Centre and the round Hamer Hall of his Arts Precinct in Melbourne.

Born in 1905, Grounds was one of Australia's pioneering modernist architects. He established himself working on homes – always with an interest in shapes, like at Grounds House, which he built for his family. It looks rectangular from the outside but hides a circular glass courtyard. His shapes were wildly experimental for the time, and the evolution of his thought and practice can be seen at a small bush site in Mimosa Rocks National Park, where Grounds would retreat to build domes, triangles and squares out of rustic and ad hoc materials (including bin lids), which he then translated into the stone and concrete of his large commissions.

In the 1950s, he set up a firm with Robin Boyd and Frederick Romberg: together, they were the Holy Trinity of modernist architects in Australia. The trio occasionally worked collaboratively, but more often separately. They eventually split up over Grounds' work on the Arts Precinct in Melbourne, the project that, more than any other, defined his career – and is still the beating heart of the city.

H is for
Henningsen

Poul Henningsen didn't want to design a house down to the last doorknob. Even though he dabbled in designing homes, pianos and even stilts, his design career had a laser focus on lighting, which Henningsen considered to be the foundation of good design.

He was born in 1894, into a world lit by candles and gas lights. If there was a light-bulb moment in his life, it was the advent of electrical light, which thrust him, and the rooms in homes, into strong, harsh brightness. He first experimented with lamps in 1915, while studying architecture. Ten years later, in 1925, he released his famous PH lamp, which had multiple shades that diffused the bulb's electrical light. Henningsen continued to evolve his PH series for the rest of his life; his most famous version, PH 5, was launched in 1958, more than 25 years after the first iteration was released.

His most dramatic design was the Artichoke lamp, with 72 copper leaves hiding the light bulb; the whole thing looked like … well, an artichoke. It created a warm, diffused light – perfect for a selfie. The lamp was originally created for the Langelinie Pavilion in Copenhagen, a new modern building rising from the ashes of the original pavilion, which had been bombed by the Germans during World War II.

Just as Finn Juhl (p.47) lived with his chairs, Henningsen lived with his prototyped lamps until he was certain he'd gotten the designs absolutely right. He was meticulous, particular and focused, designing over 100 lamps, most of them for lighting manufacturer Louis Poulsen, who he'd started working with in 1925 when his first PH lamp was launched into the market.

Such focus and determined pursuit of perfection makes Henningsen sound like a true artiste who sat in an isolated room staring at lamps all day long. This couldn't be further from the truth. Before becoming a full-time designer, he worked as a journalist, shining a light, often unflatteringly, on Danish culture.

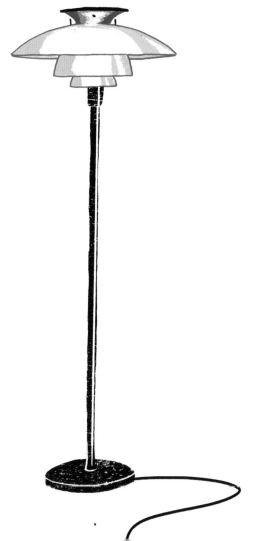

H is also for

Edith Heath

Edith Heath's ceramics are known for their distinctive glazes of deep glossy blues and terracottas. They are also enduringly beautiful, like her Coupe range with its comfortingly round lines, as illustrated to the right, or the Rim range with its coloured rims. But Heath's approach to ceramics was almost functionalist; she didn't believe in art for art's sake – it had to be *useful* and, ideally, last a lifetime. Like a true modernist, Heath didn't accept the orthodox traditions of pottery. Instead, she used a single firing of the kiln and developed her own glazes – a recognisably Heath-ian style – that she applied to her tableware and tiles.

Jorge Ferrari Hardoy

It seems to be the fate of excellent chairs – particularly mid-century modern chairs – to be widely copied. Jorge Ferrari Hardoy's Butterfly chair, designed with Antonio Bonet and Juan Kurchan, and initially known as the Hardoy Chair in America, was no exception. The trio created this slouchy slingback chair, with leather stretched between steel supports, in 1938, and in 1947 Knoll (p.48) licensed the chair and started selling it in America. Success was immediate, so much so that the market soon flooded with imitations and the licenced version couldn't compete. Knoll discontinued its production in 1950.

I is for
Indiana

If you want to see examples of some of the best work by leading mid-century modern designers, including Eero Saarinen and Alexander Girard (p.34), don't look towards the glamour of Palm Springs (p.68) or the movie-ready steel-and-glass houses of Los Angeles. Instead, turn your eyes towards … Indiana. This state has become a mecca of design thanks to one small town and one industrial giant.

The small town is Columbus, Indiana, home to only 46,000 people – yet over 60 buildings of note, including three buildings by leading mid-century modern architect Eero Saarinen, one by his father, Finnish architect Eliel Saarinen, and a bunch by Pritzker Prize winners, including I. M. Pei, Robert Venturi and Kevin Roche.

Columbus would look very different if it wasn't for J. Irwin Miller, chairman of Cummins Engine Company. Miller had two things: money and a social conscience. He'd grown up in Columbus, and wanted it to be the sort of place young, talented people would choose to live and work – and not just so that they'd work for his company, but so that the whole society would benefit. To Miller, that meant investing in great architecture.

In the 1950s, Miller noticed that there had been some shoddy school buildings constructed in town. So he told the city council that he'd stump up the cash to cover architect fees for new school buildings, as long as the council picked an architect from his pre-approved list, which was heavy with talented mid-century modern names. Top of this list? Eero Saarinen, who'd become a friend of Miller's when Eero's father, Eliel, built a church in town in the 1940s – sponsored by the Miller family, naturally.

Miller's remit soon expanded to include all public buildings and spaces in the city, including libraries and parks. Saarinen ended up designing three buildings in Columbus: Miller House, for Miller and his family; the Irwin Union Bank; and the North Christian Church, as seen in the illustration to the right. The North Christian Church is like a modernist cathedral, its sharp pyramid roof topped by a spire reaching toward the heavens.

It's almost unheard of: Miller used some of his company's profits to make the town a better place for everyone. His program inspired other leading citizens of Columbus, Indiana, to support architecture and public art. The town is now one of the best places to visit in America – if you want to look at architecture, of course.

I is also for

Iittala

Some of the biggest names in Finnish design made glassware for Iittala – Aino and Alvar Aalto (p.8), Kaj Franck (p.30), Tappio Wirkkala (p. 99), Timo Sarpaneva. Iittala started out as a small glassware factory in 1881. By the 1930s it was one of the companies leading the revolution in Finnish design. It was modernist but incredibly local, functional but still decorative – oh, and widely affordable and accessible.

Iittala supported local designers, often through competitions. One of its most influential glass ranges, Aino Aalto's Bölgeblick series of glasses and vases, was created for an Iittala competition in 1932; inspired by the ripples created when you throw a stone into water – although slightly more colourful, as seen in the illustration to the right – it was functional, stackable, and hasn't been out of production since.

Maija Isola

Big, bold poppies in pink, orange and black; huge polka dots; bulbous circles in monochrome. Maija Isola's fun, forward-thinking, graphic patterns painted Marimekko as one of Finland's, and the world's, leading textile companies. Just like her patterns, Isola's life was big, bold and unconventional, spanning numerous romantic relationships and countries. The only consistent pattern was her dedication to her art; she designed for Marimekko for 38 years and produced 500 patterns.

Isola's poppy fabric – Unikko, designed in 1964 – is Marimekko's most famous pattern. But Unikko only came about because Isola, creative and rebellious, didn't like having restrictions placed upon her. Armi Ratia, Marimekko's owner and creative director, announced that she would never print any flower patterns, as nothing could rival their beauty in nature. Isola disagreed and created a series of flower patterns. They were so spectacular, Ratia put eight into production – many still sold today.

J is for

Jacobsen

Don't let the fact that Arne Jacobsen looked like an avuncular figure – with his neat suit, neat glasses and neat hair, a pipe tucked into his mouth – fool you. He was rigorous and demanding, some might say a bully, when it came to executing his visions. His visions, luckily, were generally great, and include Aarhus City Hall, the SAS Royal Hotel, the Bellevue seaside resort and St Catherine's College at the University of Oxford.

Jacobsen was born in Copenhagen in 1902, studied architecture at the Royal Danish Academy of Fine Arts, and lived and worked in Denmark (except for a forced exile during World War II, when, being Jewish, he fled from the occupying German forces). Even though he is now considered the leading Danish architect of the 20th century, many of his projects caused outrage and controversy – a local Danish newspaper once called for him to be banned from architecture for life due to his concrete functionalist design for Stelling House in the historical centre of Copenhagen.

As the memory of public outrage fades, Jacobsen's buildings remain. In fact, they are among the most lauded in the world. Consider the illustration to the right. Have you ever seen a more attractive petrol station? Usually a concrete and neon afterthought, this petrol station on the outskirts of Copenhagen is more like a designer bathroom, covered in gleaming white tiles. This element of surprising delight is typical of Jacobsen's work.

He was an adherent of the concept of *gesamtkunstwerk*, where the architect designed everything from the building to the door handles, and believed in architecture above all else. His SAS Royal Hotel in Copenhagen, opened in 1960, was the first 'designer' hotel. It was the tallest skyscraper in Copenhagen at the time, and Jacobsen (or, more accurately, Jacobsen's office) designed everything from the building frame down to the cutlery. While the building looks like a kid's drawing of a tower – an oblong stuck in the ground – the furnishings were curvy, comfortable, dramatic. It was for this project that Jacobsen designed his Egg, possibly his most famous design, an elegantly rounded chair that embraces the person sitting in it.

Throughout his career, Jacobsen worked to create the best possible design down to the smallest teaspoon, even at the expense of public opinion – which is now on his side, anyway.

J is also for

Pierre Jeanneret

Le Corbusier (p.52) had grand ideas, but his cousin and lifelong collaborator, Pierre Jeanneret, was often responsible for making them happen. It was Jeanneret who worked closely with Charlotte Perriand (p.88) in the furniture division of Le Corbusier's studio, designing the now iconic range of furniture, including the LC4 lounge chair. It was Jeanneret, again, who actually lived in Chandigarh (p.18), developing Le Corbusier's master plan and working with Drew (p.23) and Fry on the details of building a new modernist city.

Even though Jeanneret's name is intrinsically linked with Le Corbusier's, he had a life away from his cousin. He designed his own furniture line, which included the Model 92 Scissors chair (1939), which, frankly, deserves to be more famous than it is; joined the French Resistance in World War II; and developed most of the housing in Chandigarh and stayed on as Chief Architect after the city was built. His mass-produced chairs for the city, made from temperature-resistant rattan, have now become collectors' items and sell for ridiculous sums of cash.

Philip Johnson

Many credit Johnson with bringing the ideals of modernism (and the people behind them) to America.

Born in 1906 in Ohio, Johnson studied at Harvard University. He joined the architecture department at MoMA in 1930, where he organised exhibitions introducing European modernism to America and visits by leading modernists like Le Corbusier (p.52), Mies van der Rohe and Breuer.

Johnson started his architecture practice after World War II. Inspired by Mies van der Rohe's glass Farnsworth House (p.28), one of Johnson's first buildings was a glass house called – the Glass House. But, unlike Mies van der Rohe, Johnson didn't get sued for his efforts, and wasn't plagued with quite so many problems, probably because he was both the architect and the client. His Glass House is now an American classic.

During his career, Johnson worked on many major projects, including the master plan for New York's Lincoln Centre and Seagram Building. His work was recognised when he won architecture's leading prize, the Pritzker, in 1979.

Finn Juhl

When you think about mid-century modern chairs, you might visualise the classic shapes of American designers like the Eameses – simple bucket seats and comfortable reclining chaises. In Denmark, however, chairs took on unusual forms, shapes and colours. At the forefront of this design movement, producing chairs that were sometimes too radical for the market, was architect and furniture designer Finn Juhl.

Juhl's chairs are a study of colour and comfort in sculptural form: some chairs are simple with a recognisable shape, like his 108 chair or his Japan chair, illustrated above; some are almost animalistic, like the soft Pelican chair, with a curved headrest that looks primed to take flight. He was often inspired by artworks, perhaps as a result of his childhood dream to become an art historian. Born in 1912, Juhl studied architecture at the Royal Danish Academy of Fine Arts in Copenhagen before working for architect Vilhem Lauritzen on big projects including Copenhagen Airport.

He started designing furniture in the late 1930s, measuring his own body to work out how a chair should shape to the human form, and collaborating with cabinetmaker Niels Vodder to make the chairs. They exhibited at the local Cabinetmakers' Guild shows, where they won multiple awards, leading Juhl to set up his own studio in 1945, where he focused on furniture and interior design.

K is for

Knoll

This is and it isn't about a furniture company.

It's about Knoll, the furniture company that helped commercialise mid-century modern design; it's about Florence and Hans Knoll, the people who founded and grew that company; but it's also specifically about Florence Knoll, the designer who ran the Knoll Planning Division and changed the way that people lived and worked. Yup, true to the form of mid-century modern design, this entry touches upon a little bit of everything.

Hans Knoll established Knoll in 1938, and released its first furniture line in 1942, which was mainly designed by Jens Risom (p.78). But it was Florence Knoll, having started working for the company in 1943 before marrying Hans in 1946, who positioned the company at the forefront of design through her collaborations with leading designers, like Wegner (p.96), Bertoia, Mies van der Rohe and Saarinen, as well as through her design of office spaces with the Knoll Planning Unit.

Florence attended high school in Cranbrook, becoming friends with the Saarinen family and eventually studying under Eliel Saarinen at Cranbrook Academy of Art before completing further study with Ludwig Mies van der Rohe at the Illinois Institute of Technology.

She asked Eero Saarinen (the architect behind three of the buildings in Columbus, p.40, and the TWA Flight Center, p.84) to design tables and chairs for Knoll. His designs included the space-agey white Tulip chair, with its plastic pedestal base and seat that unfurled like a flower. Florence convinced Mies van der Rohe to licence his Barcelona chair (co-designed with Lilly Reich) to Knoll. She also talked Anni Albers (p.10) into creating a textile pattern that could be mass-produced as upholstery. And, when the company needed a modern and fuss-free furniture line for offices, Florence designed it herself. This was all complemented by her husband's skills as a salesman.

When Hans died in a car crash in 1955, Florence continued running the company, growing it in size and design influence. She sold the company in 1959 and retired from Knoll in 1965. But we can thank Florence, at least in part, for making mid-century modern furniture widely available and widely influential.

K is also for

Louis Kahn

Louis Kahn was an eccentric among eccentrics, a man who wanted to use modern materials to create modern marvels of architecture. Not for him the simple lines of modernism or the functionalism of the Bauhaus. No – he wanted to create new Taj Mahals, contemporary pyramids, buildings to overawe the senses.

He was born in 1901 in what is now Estonia, and migrated to America in 1906. There, Kahn's incredible talent in art and music was recognised, and he won a scholarship to the University of Pennsylvania to study architecture. Despite his child prodigy–like abilities, Kahn was a late bloomer – which can probably be blamed on the Great Depression making it very hard for architects to get jobs. He didn't get his first major commission until 1951, when he was asked to design an extension to Yale University Art Gallery. His most famous building, the Salk Institute, looks like a medieval city – a large stone building around a central courtyard overlooking a cliff. That one wasn't finished until 1965.

Poul Kjærholm

Poul Kjærholm was a rarity in Denmark – a trained carpenter who preferred to work with steel over wood. He was an artist, and so didn't make this decision because steel was easier to work with, but because of the way that light played on the metal.

After training as a carpenter, Kjærholm attended Denmark's famous School of Arts and Crafts, where he later became a lecturer. After graduating, he started designing furniture – mainly chairs, couches and tables – always working to create objects that showed the 'truth' of their materials. His most famous chair is the PK22 chair, with a steel frame covered in slim leather that's almost like a sling-back, albeit one that looks like it could sit in the middle of a white room and be lauded as a piece of art. He also designed the PK58 table, with its distinctive steel cube frame, and the PK31/3 sofa, as illustrated above.

Pierre Koenig

Pierre Koenig's surviving buildings are more famous than he is, particularly his Stahl House (p.80), a remarkable steel-and-glass home that cantilevers from the Hollywood Hills above Los Angeles. Yet even with Stahl House on his resumé, Koenig didn't receive a huge number of commissions across his career; he only designed 43 buildings.

Stahl House, and Koenig's previous building, Bailey House, both featured in *Art & Architecture's* Case Study Houses Program (p.16), and showcased Koenig's pioneering use of steel for the frames of these homes.

His calling card as an architect was his experimentation, not just with steel, but also with passive ventilation, ideas he developed over his 40 years teaching at the University of Southern California. He designed his homes to heat and cool themselves before it was fashionable to do so. Unfortunately, people were more interested in installing air-conditioning.

William Krisel

Although William Krisel designed the House of Tomorrow, where Elvis and Priscilla Presley stayed on their honeymoon, most of his houses were not flashy or destined for American royalty. Instead, Krisel and his partner, Dan Palmer, took desert modernism – a style of modernism designed with consideration to the shimmering heat – and turned it into housing estates.

Krisel was born in Shanghai in 1924, where his father was the sole distributor of all the big Hollywood films into Asia, before moving to Los Angeles in 1937. After studying architecture at the University of Southern California and establishing his career in Los Angeles, Krisel was invited to design a new housing estate in Palm Springs (p.68) that would take the flashy Hollywood glamour of big modernist homes and make it available to ordinary Americans. This estate – the Twin Palms subdivision – changed the look of Palm Springs forever. Even though all of the homes in the estate had the same floorplan (and two palm trees out the front), with open-plan living spaces and floor-to-ceiling windows opening the homes to the outdoors, Krisel ensured the estate remained vibrant by changing the rooflines, facade colours and placements off the street. During his career, he designed numerous housing developments for a very simple reason – Krisel believed that good, affordable architecture would make life more enjoyable for everyone. Who can argue with that?

L is for
Le Corbusier

Charles-Édouard Jeanneret, or, as he called himself, Le Corbusier, was the defining architect of the 20th century. His ideas about how cities should be planned, homes should be designed, furniture should be used and ultimately how people should live, continue to exert a huge influence.

Yet he was also a problematic figure who discouraged women from working in design, vandalised Eileen Gray's house (p.32), had far-right leanings (he attempted to get commissions from the Vichy collaborationist government in France during World War II), believed in the vision of the architect above all else — and often bullied people into accepting that vision.

Le Corbusier, born in Switzerland in 1887, started out designing conventional houses. He rapidly moved towards a more modern interpretation, producing his famous adjoining Villa La Roche and Villa Jeanneret in Paris and Villa Savoye in Poissy, based on his Five Points of Architecture theory about how modernist homes should be built.

He loved a theory, often throwing ideas into the public arena to spark a conversation (and probably get publicity too), like his idea to bulldoze half of Paris and replace it with a collection of blocky towers. In 1928 he co-founded CIAM (Congrès internationaux d'architecture moderne), an organisation of modernist architects who established the principles of modernist design. CIAM wanted architecture to be used for social good by improving living quarters and city planning. Their Athens Charter (1933), which outlined how to design a modern, functional city, was inspired — of course — by one of Le Corbusier's theories.

These grand ideas influenced the planning of new cities like Chandigarh (p.18) and Brasília (p.12), as well as housing estates across England, France, Germany and America, including the Barbican in London. Some of these were epic failures — indeed, a number have been demolished — while some still remain, like Le Corbusier's own Cité radieuse in Marseilles.

He was a contradiction and a contrarian, a critic and a rabble-rouser, a humanist and a machine-loving industrialist. His ambitious, revolutionary and polarising ideas are writ in concrete across the world. The majority of well-known 20th century architects and designers, including many in this book, were connected to, and influenced by, Le Corbusier in some way. Perhaps no other designer has ever had as much global impact — a marker of his talent, and his excellent networking skills.

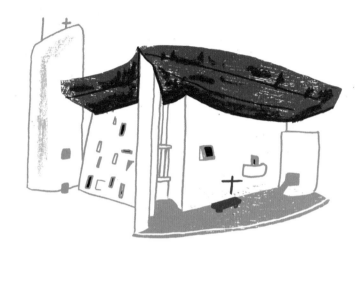

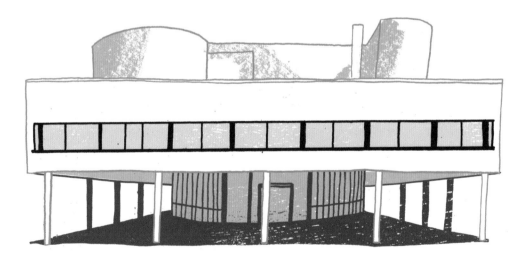

L is also for

John Lautner

If Louis Kahn (p.50) developed public buildings to be modern marvels like the pyramids, then John Lautner often designed homes to a similar effect — his buildings have been likened to volcanic caves or even spaceships, such as Chemosphere, illustrated to the right. His most famous houses are almost villainous — concrete constructions of fantastic shapes that look like futuristic bunkers. One of his homes, Elrod House in Los Angeles, was actually used as a Bond villain's home in *Diamonds are Forever*.

Born in 1911, Lautner was a disciple of Frank Lloyd Wright, and worked as one of Lloyd Wright's Taliesin Fellows in Wisconsin. Lautner moved to Los Angeles, where he continued to collaborate with Lloyd Wright (often as a problem solver), while establishing his own practice. You can see the influence of Lloyd Wright's organic architecture in Lautner's work; even though Lautner's homes are often concrete monoliths, they all have surprising openings and interactions with nature. Lest you think that Lautner was concrete-obsessed, always working on feats of astounding engineering, he also designed more subtle timber homes, like Walstrom House in the Santa Monica mountains, as well as curvy and poppy coffee shops. He was an architect who didn't stick to a particular style, but made his own.

Jacqueline Lecoq

Jacqueline Lecoq, along with her lifetime collaborator, Antoine Philippon, sought to make economical, functional furniture that could be mass-produced — if it was also beautiful, so much the better. The pair are perhaps most famous for their President desk, which almost looks like a steel-and-glass Case Study House (p.16) turned into a table.

Lecoq was born in 1932, and started designing furniture after World War II, joining the radical French Union of Modern Artists. This group rejected traditional, aspirationally ornamental furniture, and actively designed items to *not* look rich, but to form simple, practical and straightforward shapes using modern materials.

She met Philippon in the early 1950s at the studio of Marcel Gascoin, a rationalist designer who believed that designers should make objects that have a reason, a function, and that could be accessible to most people. This idea — along with Jean Prouvé's (p.70) ideas about producing truly useful items — influenced Lecoq and Philippon, although you wouldn't know it by the prices their furniture sells at today.

M is for
Materials

To build the future, you need materials. And not just any materials – these materials need to be available, affordable, long-lasting and able to be mass-produced. Materials made mid-century modern design; that, and the successes, failures and wild experimentation of the architects and designers working in this era.

The defining items of the era – from the Eameses' (p.24) famous plywood designs to Robin Day's (p.20) stackable polypropylene chairs, from the curvy plastic lamps of Vico Magistretti (p.58) to Donald Wexler's (p.99) replicable steel frames in Palm Springs – would not have been possible without the availability of new materials and new techniques for using them, some of which were developed during World War II.

One of the most famous chairs in the world was only possible due to advances in materiality. The Eameses' plastic chair, the chair that launched a thousand replications and imitations, was the culmination of Charles Eames' long-held desire to produce a single-shell chair that could be mass-produced. After Charles' early experiments with plywood shells, the Eameses tried steel, but it was too expensive. Then they experimented with plastic – specifically, glass-fibre reinforced polyester resin. It worked, and by 1950, they had produced the world's first mass-producible plastic chair.

Robin Day – our Festival Hall chair-man extraordinaire, one part of England's dream design couple – similarly came up with a simple, stackable single-shell chair made out of polypropylene, a material which had only been invented in 1954.

This new materiality not only applied to furniture, but also to homes. In France, designers like Jean Prouvé (p.71) experimented with building demountable shelters and homes from steel; in America, architects like Pierre Koenig (p.51) played with using glass and steel to design homes for the modern family; although it took Donald Wexler (p.99), working on a subdivision in Palm Springs (p.68), to come up with a truly replicable and prefabricated plan for a steel-framed house.

Using steel, plastic, timber and concrete, mid-century modern architects designers constructed a new world where good design was a consumer good – and looked great.

M is also for

Greta Magnusson-Grossman

When Greta Magnusson-Grossman moved to America from Sweden in 1940 with her jazz musician husband, she arrived with pizzazz, announcing to the local paper that documented her arrival that she wanted to buy shorts and a car – the only purchases you needed to be modern in America. She'd already achieved success in Sweden with a similar level of panache. She was the first woman to win an award for furniture design from the Stockholm Craft Association, and established her own studio, aptly called Studio, in the early 1930s, which became a gathering place for young, cool, sceney and edgy creatives.

But Magnusson-Grossman didn't just have personal style – her work had it too, like the desk illustrated to the right. Her most famous design, the Cobra lamp, was one of the first lamps to have a flexible arm with a curvy, irregular lampshade. It was sexy, a mash-up of Scandinavian simplicity and originality with a little dash of Californian fun. It's no wonder she was in such high demand, not just as an industrial designer, but also as an architect and interior designer. She experienced rapid and heady success in Los Angeles, becoming interior designer to stars like Greta Garbo, before, like Garbo, retiring and retreating to the country, where she was mainly forgotten.

Vico Magistretti

Magistretti sits alongside Gio Ponti (p.71) as one of the most important Italian designers of the 20th century. His extensive body of work across buildings, chairs, lamps, city planning and teaching influenced students, cities and the sort of chairs people sit on. Inspired by his mentor, humanist architect Ernesto Roberts, as well as by the other members of CIAM, the organisation that formalised the principles of modernist design, Magistretti subscribed to the thought that design should contribute to the greater good.

But even though you can see these principles in his buildings, like Torre al Parco in Milan and the Carimate golf club near Como, it's clear that Magistretti established his own design approach, away from someone else's rules. He wanted to design useful appliances – he had fruitful relationships with furniture company Cassina and lighting company Artemide – that eschewed unnecessary decoration. But he also had *fun*. His industrial designs were colourful, playful, modern in materials and approach. His most famous lamp, the Eclisse, is a round plastic lamp with a revolving shade that periodically blocks out the light ... kind of like an eclipse.

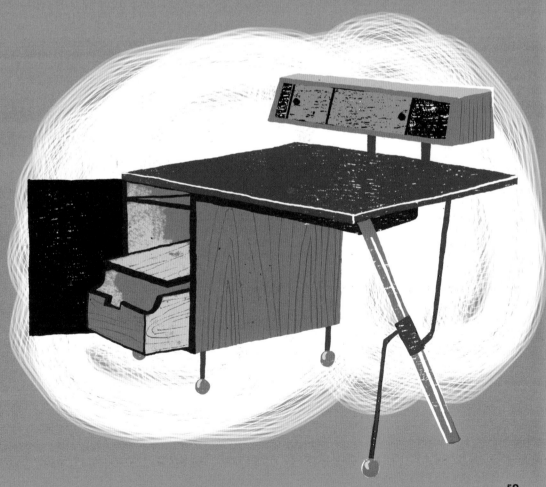

N is for
Nelson

In its mid-century heyday, Herman Miller was one of the leading manufacturers of modern design in America. Its furniture was inventive, it used new materials like plastic, and it was *fun*. There were starburst clocks, couches that looked like marshmallows, chairs named after coconuts. The man behind it all was George Nelson, who had an eye and a nose for designs that people wanted to buy. In fact, Nelson's time as the design director of Herman Miller was one of the defining periods of mid-century modern design – and it came about because of one good idea.

Nelson was born in 1908 in Hartford, Connecticut, and studied architecture at Yale University – apparently because he'd stumbled into the architecture building as a teenager and liked what he saw. After graduating, he established himself as an architect and a leading design critic. His book, *Tomorrow's House*, had more than a catchy title. It had persuasive ideas about how homes could be better designed, including the Storagewall – a forward-thinking concept for turning the forgotten space between walls into storage. This one good idea set off a media flurry, which caught the attention of D.J. De Pree, founder and owner of Herman Miller. De Pree travelled to New York and hired George Nelson as his director of design, spurring Nelson to set up his own design studio at the same time.

Along with an eye for design, Nelson had an eye for talent. He hired people like Irving Harper to work for his studio, producing designs for all manner of objects, both for Herman Miller and other clients. Of course, these objects were released under the name of George Nelson, rather than the person who designed them – the clocks to the right were actually designed by Harper, not Nelson. But Nelson understood the power of branding. It couldn't be Irving Harper for George Nelson for Herman Miller – that's just bad business.

Alongside the work that his studio produced for Herman Miller, Nelson also recruited major designers like Charles and Ray Eames (p.24), Isamu Noguchi (p.63) and Alexander Girard (p.34) to design furniture for the company.

More than just a designer, Nelson had a seemingly endless stream of good ideas that, beyond his work in shaping the homes and offices of America through Herman Miller, extended to architecture theory and criticism, as well as designs for homes, interiors and lives.

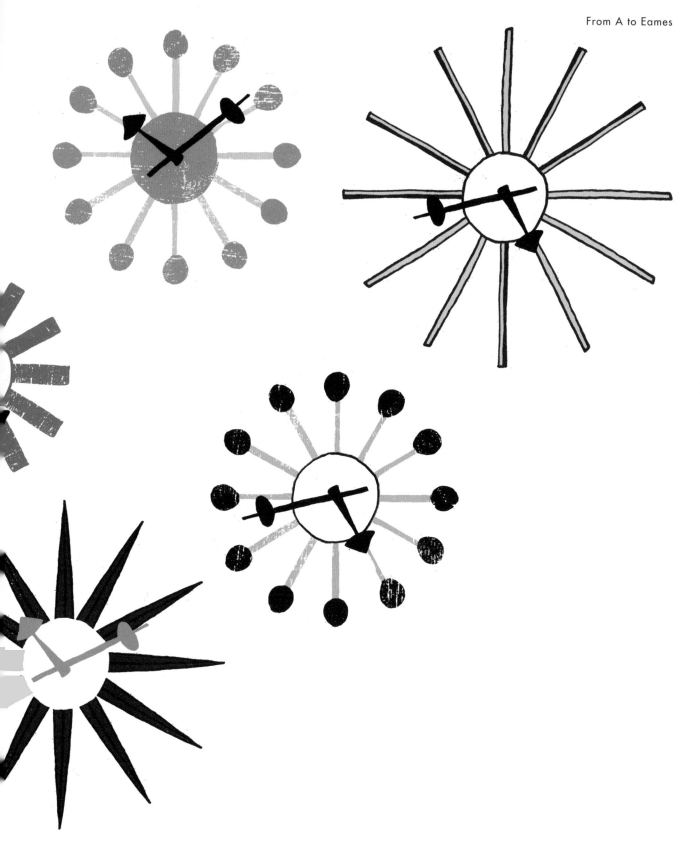

N is also for

George Nakashima

George Nakashima believed in the integrity of materials, particularly in a good piece of timber, which meant that no two pieces of furniture he made were ever the same. He became famous for this furniture, for his distinctive bench seats that look like you're sitting on a cross-section of a tree – albeit one with back support – and his beautifully rough-hewn tables.

You might think that Nakashima had always been drawn to wood, but he didn't dedicate his time to woodworking until after World War II. Born in Washington to Japanese parents, he studied architecture at the University of Washington and MIT. After graduating, he travelled the world. He ended up in Tokyo, where he worked with prominent American architect Antonin Raymond, who was busy designing the iconic Four Seasons hotel, as well as other buildings around Asia.

Nakashima returned to America in 1940, but was imprisoned in an internment camp for Japanese-Americans in 1942. Here he learnt traditional Japanese joinery techniques from a fellow detainee. He was sponsored for release by Raymond and subsequently moved to Raymond's property in New Farm, Pennsylvania, where Nakashima focused on furniture. Not just any furniture, though – wood furniture, furniture that tells a story through its knots and burls.

Richard Neutra

Richard Neutra did more than just design modern homes of steel, glass and timber; he took modernism, and made it Californian. His buildings represented the Californian dream, an easy-breezy way of living that was about open-plan spaces, a connection with nature, and, if possible, great views.

He wasn't modern simply for the sake of it. He wanted his houses to help people live better, whether that was through incorporating passive heating to cope with the blistering sun, or by designing a modern house that – shockingly – was suited to the needs of each client, like his house for Constance Perkins, planned for her small stature and her similarly small budget. He didn't design houses and then move on, but was famous for popping by his creations years later.

Yet Neutra is most famous for the houses he made for clients with large budgets, such Kaufmann House in Palm Springs, designed for department store magnate Edgar J. Kaufmann in 1946; and the multi-storey Lovell House which was the first steel house in America when it was built in 1929 and established Neutra's reputation as one of California's leading modernist architects.

Neutra became synonymous with this new style of modernism, so much so that he featured on the cover of *Time* magazine in 1949 with the heading: 'What will the neighbours think?' If they had any sense, they'd be jealous.

Isamu Noguchi

If you've ever seen a paper lamp from IKEA, chances are it was inspired by Isamu Noguchi, a sculpture artist who created buildings, furniture and public art. Noguchi approached all his designs as if they were sculptures — just look at his Akari Light Sculptures, the lamps illustrated above, inspired by Japanese paper artists. He created the first two lamps in Gifu — a town in Japan famous for its production of paper parasols — using paper, washi tape and bamboo. This line eventually expanded to hanging lamps, wall lamps and floor lamps, in all different shapes and sizes.

Noguchi was born in 1904 to an American mother and a Japanese father, though he got little from his dad apart from his last name. He spent his childhood travelling with his mother between Japan and America. While Noguchi is now more well known for his lamps and Vitra's iconic Noguchi coffee table — its three-legged wooden base looks more like a sculpture than table legs — he was also an artist. He created pieces noted for their bold materiality, like his sculpture above the entrance to the Rockefeller Center in New York. Between his prolific work as an artist and industrial designer, he was also a prolific activist, particularly when he shone a light on the internment of Japanese-Americans in camps throughout World War II.

O is for

Organic chair

The Organic chair was an award-winning failure. It was designed by Charles Eames (p.24) and Eero Saarinen – two young architects who'd met at Cranbrook Academy of Art – for MoMA's *Organic Designs in Mass Furnishings* competition in 1940.

The design that Eames and Saarinen put forward for this competition looked and felt modern; it featured an experimental moulded three-dimensional plywood frame in a single shell, with no extra ornamentation or decoration. But the chair was so modern that factories didn't have the technology to mass-produce it – one of the key judging criteria of the competition, which aimed to put the winning designs into mass production and hopefully into homes around America.

In all other respects, the chair met the brief and won the 'Seating for the Living Room' category. The competition had been organised to encourage more modern furniture that would reflect how people lived in the modern age, with minimal ornamentation and fuss – just like the Organic chair.

Even though it was initially a commercial failure, the Organic chair was highly influential, and its simple form inspired both Eames and Saarinen, in their separate practices, in the following years. Charles, married to artist Ray, spent the early 1940s working with Ray on plywood designs for the war effort, including a moulded plywood splint for injured soldiers. This experimentation enabled them to finally produce the LCM chair, a plywood chair with a curved back and seat that were joined with either a steel or plywood rod. This chair could be easily mass-produced, although it still wasn't the single-shell chair that Charles had dreamed of.

It wasn't until fibreglass plastic became widely available for manufacturing after the war that the Eameses (and subsequently Saarinen) were able to mass-produce single-shell chairs. The Organic chair is now in production as originally designed.

O is also for

Opdahl House

You might call John Entenza, editor of *Arts & Architecture* magazine, the kingmaker of mid-century modern architects. He influenced the careers of numerous architects through his Case Study Houses Program (p.16) – Edward Killingsworth, the architect of Opdahl House, included. Entenza had driven by the home that Killingsworth had designed for his in-laws; Entenza liked what he saw, and invited Killingsworth to contribute to the Case Study Houses Program. Killingsworth came up with six Case Study Houses, four of which were built.

Opdahl House, which was built in Long Beach in 1957 and illustrated below, won a number of awards, including the AIA National Honor Award and the Architectural Record of Excellence. It's not a large space, but includes features for which Killingsworth became known, such as double-height living spaces and large windows. He designed places intended to make the spirit soar. Looking out from Opdahl House's double-height living room through the double-height windows onto the reflective pool between the house and carport – with this design, he succeeded.

Olivetti

In the 1960s Olivetti, an Italian typewriter company established in 1908, ushered in the future to the clattering sound of their cutting-edge typewriters, calculators and computers. But these products weren't just pioneering in terms of technology, but also in design – sleek, colourful and cool devices that sprang from the minds of some of Italy's leading industrial designers, like Ettore Sottsass and Mario Bellini. In this era, Olivetti was in the business of good design, and good design *was* good business.

Their commitment to good design extended to their factories. They hired architects like Louis Kahn (p.50) to create soaring factories that would look good *and* improve the lives of Olivetti's employees, before the term 'work-life balance' existed. Olivetti took this idea even further when they attempted to turn Ivrea – the Italian town where they had their headquarters – into the ideal modern city, a workers' paradise that included free summer camps, cultural programs, a staff library and a free medical clinic. Oh, and their stores were pretty snazzy too.

P is for
Palm Springs

Ah, Palm Springs in the 1950s, a time when you might find Frank Sinatra literally running up a flag at his E. Stewart Williams' designed home, Twin Palms, to invite the neighbours over for a cocktail by the pool. While the era of Hollywood stars escaping to Palm Springs for the weekend might have passed, the mid-century modern homes that they lived in remain (as does the town's cocktail-making skills, we assume).

It was a time that has gone down in myth and legend, not purely for the excesses of the Hollywood weekenders, but for the architectural experimentation. Palm Springs was where John Lautner (p.54) built Elrod House, a concrete spaceship of a home that overlooks Coachella Valley; it was also where Albert Frey built himself a glass house around a rock in the mountains, wanting it to appear part of the landscape. It was the place where Richard Neutra (p.62) became the successor to Frank Lloyd Wright when Edgar J. Kaufmann, department store magnate and house-proud owner of Lloyd Wright's masterpiece Fallingwater, commissioned Neutra to build him a holiday house. Neutra produced desert modernist showstopper Kaufmann House, which looks like it grew out of the sand and stone of the desert. Even the city council jumped on board, hiring modern architects to construct public buildings, like the city's airport, designed by Donald Wexler (p.98).

During this mythical era, with the hazy-warm glow of a desert morning over it, mid-century modern homes in Palm Springs were going up by the thousands; not just for Hollywood stars and industry magnates, but for regular people in new housing developments. It was a lifestyle that you could literally buy into, open-plan living and palm trees included.

The most famous subdivision in Palm Springs was Twin Palms — coincidentally the same name as Sinatra's house. Each house featured two palms out the front, letting homeowners know that good times started here. Even though the houses, designed by local architect William Krisel, all followed the same floorplan, the external differences — variations of different rooflines, setbacks, and pastel colours — created a more interesting street frontage.

Today, Palm Springs appears like a mirage in the desert. It's a beacon of mid-century modern design, where the flag is always raised and it's always cocktail hour.

P is also for

Clara Porset

Clara Porset's butaque chairs are things of beauty, long, low loungers in the style of the chairs the Aaltos (p.8) created for the Paimio Sanatorium – but made in Mexico, for Mexicans, using local materials. Her designs were exceedingly popular, especially with the elite of Mexico, having pride of place in exclusive hotels as well as the home of the president. These chairs look effortless; a contrast to the effort it must have taken for Porset to establish her name in the male-dominated design field.

She was born in Cuba in 1895 to a wealthy family. She educated herself by travelling voraciously and dipping in and out of study at various design schools, with a particular interest in the ideals of the Bauhaus. She met Walter Gropius (p.34) at the Bauhaus school before it closed, and spent a summer learning from former Bauhaus teachers and artists Anni and Josef Albers (p.10) at Black Mountain College in America. Returning to Cuba, Porset established herself as a designer before the deteriorating political situation precipitated her move to Mexico.

In Mexico she designed her butaque chairs, along with a range of other furniture, some of which was put into production by Mexican manufacturers. Luis Barragán (p.15) also asked her to create furniture for his houses. Wherever Porset went, she mixed with the elite; never more so than when she returned to Cuba and was invited by Fidel Castro to create furniture and open a School of Industrial Design. The school didn't eventuate; the political situation in Cuba once again deteriorated. Porset returned to Mexico and continued designing.

Panthella lamp

Forget what you think you know about serious modern designers and serious metal lamps and serious leather chairs. Verner Panton designed in a different vernacular: one of colour, fun and wild shapes. His Panthella lamp – reminiscent of Magistretti's (p.58) Eclisse lamp – is illustrated above, and often called the mushroom lamp, with a domed shade that seems to sprout from its curved pedestal stand. It was designed to reflect light off every surface, to liven and lighten up spaces. When first released in 1971, the Panthella lamp came out in a variety of colours, including this bold yellow. It's all a little bit ... fun, a word that can also be applied to his iconic plastic, stackable 'S' chair.

You might not think it by looking at this lamp, but Panton was embedded in the Danish design establishment; after graduating from architecture at the Royal Danish Academy of Fine Arts, he was employed by Arne Jacobsen (p.44) for two years. He set up his own studio in 1955 and worked for a variety of manufacturers, including Louis Poulsen, for whom he designed the Panthella lamp as both a table and floor lamp.

Gio Ponti

From the sinuous curves of his La Cornuta espresso machine to the curved roof of Villa Planchart (p.94), Gio Ponti made design sexy. He also made design part of everything – there was seemingly nothing he couldn't do. He was the architect behind Milan's iconic Pirelli Tower, founded *Domus* magazine, designed the Superleggera chair and created some of the most beautiful private homes in the world. He defined a generation of Italian design, and mentored up-and-coming architects. Yes – Gio Ponti is a name you should know.

Born in Milan in 1891, Ponti studied architecture at the Polytechnic University of Milan, although his studies were interrupted by World War I, where he served on the front line. Unlike many modernists, Ponti designed with splashy colour and decoration. The facade of his Villa Planchart in Caracas is unadorned, but step inside and you enter a world of colourful artistry. He also painted murals on the walls of the Bo Palace at the University of Padua. Yet his industrial design could be plain, like his Superleggera (super light) chair, which was simple and ... super light. His body of work was diverse, exciting and still stands the test of time.

Jean Prouvé

To Jean Prouvé, design was egalitarian. He didn't design objects to be pretty, but to solve problems; and his homes and furniture were free from ornament and decoration. His most notable design was his metal demountables, which he created to house refugees after World War II. They were quick to set up, quick to take down and didn't leave a trace. Similarly, his chairs were intended for practical function, and were used in schools and other public buildings. His ideas influenced a generation of French designers, and he collaborated with other designers including Charlotte Perriand (p.88) and Pierre Jeanneret (p.46).

Prouvé grew up in an artistic household in Nancy, France: his dad an artist, his mum a pianist. He trained as a metal artisan and used steel as the foundational material for all of his designs. Prouvé mainly worked for himself, setting up a variety of studios (including a factory where the other shareholders forced Prouvé out in 1953 – business may not have been his strong suit).

Yet even as Prouvé is being rediscovered by a new generation, it shouldn't be forgotten that his influence extended beyond materials, beyond his designs. He joined the French Resistance during World War II, and became mayor of Nancy after the war ended. He was also on the panel that selected Rogers and Piano as the winning entry to design the Centre Pompidou in Paris. This man of steel changed the fabric of France and its design community.

Q is for

A. Quincy Jones

A. Quincy Jones, or Quincy, as he was commonly known, is probably most famous for designing presidential retreat Sunnylands in Palm Springs, illustrated below, a house that's like the Energiser Bunny – it just keeps going and going. One of his first commissions was to design a house for Hollywood tough-man Gary Cooper. Other Quincy homes have been owned by the likes of Jennifer Aniston and Ellen DeGeneres. It's no wonder that Quincy developed a reputation as an architect who designed large homes for large budgets.

Yet this is only part of the truth. Quincy's homes don't just dot the Hollywood Hills, but also subdivisions across California, as well as a pioneering housing co-operative in Crestwood Hills above Los Angeles. In fact, if one of the principles of mid-century modern design was to have replicable, mass-produced and affordable homes, then forget about the Eameses (p.24), Koenig (p.51) and Ellwood (p.26) – A. Quincy Jones was your guy.

He was prolific in both buildings — he designed over 5000 structures across his career — and collaborations, working with a number of other architects on public buildings and private commissions. Most notably, he worked with Whitney Smith and engineer Edgardo Contini on Crestwood Hills, where families joined together to buy their own land and fund their own modernist houses in a post–World War II housing co-operative; and with Frederick Emmons on his work with developer Joseph Eichler (p.27). The three public buildings Quincy designed for Palm Springs were collaborations with Paul R. Williams, the first African-American man admitted to the American Institute of Architects. Beyond Quincy's architectural partnerships, he also taught architecture at the University of Southern California for almost two decades.

The varying scope and scale of his work allowed Quincy to experiment with materials, as well as different ideas about better ways of living. He played around with various innovations for being environmentally responsible — way before it was cool — like the communal green spaces in his housing estates, and attempts at passive cooling in the Palm Springs houses. Quincy's motto was that there was no unimportant architecture — and if you look at his work, from the expansive modernist homes of the rich to the open-plan and warm factory-line homes of his estates, you can see his words in action.

Q is also for

Jens Quistgaard

The illustration on the opposite page shows Quistgaard's iconic nesting side tables, which are the babushka dolls of mid-century modern design. The layers of his design are an apt metaphor for his talents as a designer, where he just kept pulling more skills out of his hat, designing everything from villas to cutlery. His most well-known designs were created for Dansk Designs, which – name aside – was an American company founded by Ted Nierenberg to sell Scandinavian designs into the massive US market. Nierenberg discovered Quistgaard on a trip to Copenhagen, and convinced him to lead the design for Dansk. It was a partnership of business nous and design, in the style of D.J. De Pree and George Nelson (p.60) of Herman Miller, or Hans Knoll and Florence Knoll at Knoll (p.48).

Some of Quistgaard's designs for Dansk included Fjord cutlery, which were steel utensils with wooden handles; his range of teak pepper mills, which are now collectors' items; and his teak serving bowls. Even though Quistgaard's name is largely forgotten outside of pepper-mill collectors' circles, his designs were wildly successful and influential in America, introducing Scandi design to a new consumer group. All this from a designer with little to no formal training.

Quaderna table

Mid-century modern design changed the way people lived, worked, sat and consumed … everything. It was revolutionary. Radical design studio Superstudio, established in Milan in the 1960s, was formed with the aim of rejecting this orthodoxy, announcing that they were over tasteful 'good design'; yet their very attempt at revolution through using big ideas (and products that were big on function) was, well, very mid-century modern.

Superstudio created aggressively plain and aggressively functional furniture, like their famous Quaderna table, designed in 1970. It looks almost like the template of a table, with a flat square surface and rectangular legs, covered in white plastic laminate screenprinted with black grid lines. The white background with black grid lines became Superstudio's calling card, an ironic nod to the modernist ideals of architects like Le Corbusier who believed that everything could and should be designed to a grid, that a rational approach to street planning could make lives better – a theory Superstudio thought time had proven epically wrong.

Beyond a statement on design culture, the table is also edgy and still on-trend – and, perhaps ironically for a table that was labelled 'anti-design', now highly covetable.

R is for

Rose Seidler House

This simple, boxy house — one of Australia's first modernist homes — sits like a witch's house in a modern fairytale, a white jewel-box that can only be discovered by the brave or intrepid. At the time it was built, Rose Seidler House was located in a far, bushy outpost from the city. The way there is perhaps not quite as perilous now, marked by a small sign on a road in Sydney's endless suburbs.

Rose Seidler House was the first commission of young Harry Seidler. He was Jewish, born in Vienna, but escaped with his parents to England before World War II. Eventually he moved to America, where he studied under Walter Gropius (p.34) at Harvard University, worked with Alvar Aalto (p.8), studied some more under Josef Albers and worked for a couple of years as Marcel Breuer's assistant — not a bad start. His parents, Max and Ruth, emigrated to Australia after the war ended. It was Max and Ruth who asked their son to come to Australia and build them a house in Sydney's Wahroonga.

The influence of modernist heroes on Seidler's design are clear, from the Le Corbusier—influenced (p.52) mural on the wall of the courtyard to the house's clean white lines, inspired by his mentor, Gropius. Yet, just as a fairytale speaks to its origins and location, so too does Rose Seidler House embrace its Australian surrounds, nestled into the trees, with local sandstone used for the walls and fireplaces.

Seidler only meant to be in Australia long enough to see the house finished, but was tempted to stay because the reception to Rose Seidler House had been so positive, and he'd received numerous job offers. Plus, there was the excellent climate. His other modernist buildings, ranging from the controversial Blues Point Tower overlooking the Sydney Harbour Bridge to the MLC Centre, remain part of the city, and are a defining part of Sydney's modernist history.

R is also for

Lucie Rie

When Lucie Rie landed in London after escaping Vienna just as Austria entered into an alliance with Germany on the eve of World War II, she made ends meet by designing and making buttons from clay. This might seem an odd choice, but Rie had already established an international reputation for herself as a ceramicist; she'd set up her own studio in Vienna in 1925 after studying pottery at the Vienna School of Arts and Crafts. She glazed her pots in restrained colours of grey and white, and won multiple prizes at exhibitions around Europe. When she fled Vienna, she left behind her home, her studio, her reputation – and had to build a whole new life for herself in England.

She started making buttons for Fritz Lampl, who ran a glassware and ceramics company called Orplid, through which he gave work to refugees. Soon, Rie had established her own studio and hired an assistant. This expanded to six employees, including Hans Coper, who became her lifelong collaborator. In her hands, buttons were not the everyday, functional and almost invisible buttons on a shirt. They were decorative works of art, which she made for couture and fashion houses, matching her designs to their fabrics.

Established once again, Rie returned to pots, hand-thrown on the wheel, such as the ones illustrated below. She experimented with glazes and firing techniques, selling her creations through department stores like Heal's. Rie was a woman of and beyond her time, creating space for herself as an artist, a woman and a refugee.

Jens Risom

Hans Knoll (p.48), the scion of a wealthy German family, had moved to the US and was looking for a designer who could create interiors and furniture for his new business, Knoll. Enter Jens Risom, a newly arrived Danish designer who had studied under Kaare Klint at the Royal Danish Academy of Fine Arts in Copenhagen. Risom designed Knoll's first-ever furniture line, which was launched in a catalogue in 1942. There were two standouts among the 15 new designs: the lounge chair, which had nylon-fabric webbing for the back and seat, using parachute offcuts; and the Amoeba coffee table, a wooden table that looked like a wobbly liver. This catalogue launched Knoll with all the panache of a queen smashing a champagne bottle against a ship – a new kind of furniture royalty had arrived.

Risom left Knoll to fight in World War II. When he returned, Florence Knoll was the design director. They didn't agree on the design future of Knoll, and Risom left to start his own company with immediate and sustained success, particularly after the release of the iconic advertising campaign shot by Richard Avedon – the ads proclaimed, 'The Answer is Risom'.

Dietar Rams

Dietar Rams influenced a generation of industrial designers. In fact, the iPhone would look entirely different without the new design language and rules established by Rams throughout his tenure as design director of consumer goods company, Braun. At Braun, Rams designed everything from record players to food mixers. He mainly used plastic and steel to create products that were functional, practical and – there's really no other way to put it – super cool.

Yet, his life (and our design vernacular) could have gone in an entirely different direction. Born in Germany in 1932, Rams studied architecture at Wiesbaden School of Art, joining an architecture firm after graduating. A couple of years later, Braun advertised for an architect. Rams didn't want to apply, but was convinced by a friend. He got the job, moved into industrial design and became Braun's head of design from 1961 to 1995.

Even though he designed hundreds of products, Rams rejected fast design that would be easily tossed out by consumers. Instead, he created designs to last and be useful. In this, he was influenced by the function-first approach of architectural styles like the Bauhaus – and perhaps their materiality, as Rams' designs are heavy on steel and glass. He designed over 500 products while at Braun, including his iconic record players; he was the first to suggest that record players have transparent lids so you can see the record spinning.

Sergio Rodrigues

Sergio Rodrigues was Brazil's first big-name furniture designer, a man who took what he liked from modernism and infused it with Brazilian spirit, using Brazilian materials. His most famous design was the Mole armchair (which he designed in 1961), with a jacaranda frame and overstuffed leather cushions that oozed off the armrests as though they were in a Surrealist painting, only attached by leather straps. This furniture is not restrained; it had more in common with the sculptural furniture designs coming out of Denmark than the 'classic' shapes dominating in America. But one word you could use to describe all of his chairs? Comfortable.

He was born in 1927 in Rio de Janeiro, and graduated from architecture school in 1951. He set up a furniture shop in the mid-1950s before establishing his own studio, where he made furniture that was quickly snapped up for major buildings in Brazil's newly minted capital, Brasília (p.12), as well as for the Brazilian embassy in Rome.

S is for
Stahl House

If any building could be a supermodel, it would be Stahl House. Not only is this home graceful, with a glass living room that cantilevers over Sunset Boulevard from the Hollywood Hills, it's also incredibly photogenic, and has probably booked more ad campaigns than Naomi Campbell.

Built on a steep site, Stahl House has a long, plain windowless wall that faces the street. But walk around to the front, which faces the view, and the house is revealed: a glamorous glass L-shaped building with a pool instead of a courtyard.

When you look at Stahl House now, it doesn't seem like a crazy idea. Yet, after Bud and Carlotta Stahl bought the land for a bargain price because the site was so steep, they asked architect after architect to build them a house with a cantilevered living room. They got rejection after rejection. No one wanted to risk building such a radical design on such a steep site. No one, that is, except for Pierre Koenig (p.51), a young architect who'd proven himself to be part of the vanguard of mid-century modern design with his steel and glass design for Bailey House, otherwise known as Case Study House 21.

Bud might have had the vision, but Koenig had the talent to make it a reality, and by 1960 the house was built. When John Entenza, editor of *Arts & Architecture* magazine and the brain behind the Case Study Houses Program (p.16), heard about Stahl House, he made it Case Study House 22.

It wasn't long before the house was featured in its first photoshoot, with architectural photographer Julius Shulman (p.82) snapping away for *Arts & Architecture* magazine. His photo is an iconic frame of the era: two women, illuminated by lamps, sitting in the living room and looking out over Los Angeles glittering far below. Today the photo evokes nostalgia for a time when a plucky young family could partner with a plucky young architect to create a house that looks like a million dollars.

The Stahls, whose children still own the house, lived in it for the rest of their lives – an ordinary family in an extraordinary modern home, living the dream that John Entenza, through his Case Study Houses Program, had had for the rest of America.

S is also for

Julius Shulman

Picture this: two glamorous women in cocktail dresses sitting in a glass living room that cantilevers off a cliff, with the lights of Los Angeles shining far below. They are paused in a moment, drinks in hand; at the time, they looked achingly modern. This is Pierre Koenig's Stahl House (p.80), as photographed by Julius Shulman, the man whose images immortalised mid-century modern design.

Born in Brooklyn in 1910, Shulman moved to Los Angeles when he was 12, taking his first photographs as a teenager. When he dropped out of electrical engineering at university and was bumming around Los Angeles, a friend working in Richard Neutra's office invited Shulman to come and see Neutra's recently completed Kun House. Shulman snapped some photos, which Neutra saw and liked – that was the beginning of Shulman as mid-century modern architecture's leading photographer.

He opened his own studio in 1950, and photographed all of the leading modernist homes. His work was the best advertisement for the designs of the era (and in some instances the only record of now demolished houses).

Small Homes Service

If the Case Study Houses Program (p.16) was meant to show how materials like steel and plastic could be used to build replicable modernist homes, the Small Homes Service went one step further. Created by leading Australian architect Robin Boyd in collaboration with the Victorian arm of the Australian Institute of Architects, the Small Homes Service made house plans by leading modernist architects available to anyone for a small fee of £5 (they came complete with working drawings and specifications). Each plan was designed to be built for under £1000.

For the first few years, an estimated 20 per cent of all new homes in Melbourne, Australia, were built using plans from the Small Homes Service. The scheme ran for 20 years, and featured contributions from 30 leading architects, with 200 house options between them. This project aligned with Boyd's voracious scholarship, particularly his idea of the 'Australian ugliness' – homes designed without respect to landscape, climate or community. The Small Homes Service aimed to combat this, to create a new style of house that was designed for the Australian climate – and would make for more attractive suburbs, too.

Raphael Soriano

Raphael Soriano was the good friend of Julius Shulman (p.82), who designed the photographer's long rectangular glass home in Los Angeles, illustrated below.

Born in Rhodes in 1904, Soriano immigrated to America in 1924 and studied architecture at the University of Southern California. He became immersed in the local architecture community, completing internships with Richard Neutra (p.62) and Neutra's old friend, Rudolf Schindler. Just like Neutra, Soriano was a pioneering and award-winning architect whose buildings have been widely demolished; sadly, only a handful now remain. In his time, he was wildly experimental, particularly with steel; he built one of the first steel-framed houses for the Case Study Houses Program (p.16), and worked with developer Joseph Eichler (p.27) to build a steel-framed house that could be mass-produced. These, and his other remaining houses, are mainly found in San Francisco, and are highly sought after.

T is for

TWA Flight Center

Of all the buildings designed by Finnish-American architect Eero Saarinen, the TWA Flight Center at John F. Kennedy International Airport in New York is probably the most iconic, even though it's no longer used as an airport. A bulbous building with wings, it looks like a bird, or maybe a plane. In fact, the whole building seems almost ready to lift off the ground. It's joyous and optimistic – a physical representation of the enthusiasm around air travel when the building opened in 1962.

It's this reaching, this excitement, that characterises Saarinen's buildings; he used modern ideas and modern techniques to represent the possibilities of the era, much like the soaring arch of his St Louis Gateway, or the piercing spire of the North Christian Church in Columbus, Indiana (p.40), or even the plastic unfurling of his Tulip chair.

Saarinen is one of the pivotal figures in mid-century modern design. His life was defined by the connections that tied so many of the designers and architects of this era together. His dad was pioneering Finnish architect Eliel Saarinen, who moved the whole family to America so he could teach (and eventually run) Cranbrook Academy of Art, where Charles and Ray Eames (p.24) met, Florence Knoll (p.48) hung out, and the budding ideas of the mid-century modern era bloomed. Saarinen also studied at the academy, becoming a friend and collaborator of Charles Eames (as well as the Organic chair, p.64, they also designed Entenza House together, which sits next to Eames House in Pacific Palisades in Los Angeles), before joining Eliel's architecture firm.

By the time he was asked to design the TWA Flight Center, he'd branched away from his father and established an impressive career for himself. The center was one of his final designs, as he died unexpectedly in 1961. Just like Stahl House (p.80), the TWA Flight Center captured the spirit of an era – a time when a big idea could take flight: like a plane, a design era or an architecturally experimental airport terminal. Saarinen's buildings (and his furniture, designed for Knoll, p.48), perhaps more than any other designer's, represent the soaring ideals and material possibilities of the mid-century modern era.

T is also for

Ralph Tubbs

In his design of the Dome of Discovery, illustrated below, and master plan for 1951's Festival of Britain, Ralph Tubbs was representing the brightness of Britain's future. The festival was an optimistic endeavour, commissioned by the Clem Atlee Labour government to invigorate the British public at the end of rationing, one of the hangovers from World War II. It celebrated Britain's past and present achievements, and anticipated future successes. Tubbs' dome was one of the main attractions, a gleaming futuristic steel dome that was 365 feet in diameter – big enough to fit a life-sized reproduction of Captain Cook's *Endeavour*.

It was a big idea and big in execution, which was appropriate for Tubbs, who was an ideas man. Apart from being one of Britain's leading architects – his work can be seen all over the UK from the Charing Cross Hospital in London to the iconic Granada Studios in Manchester, where the Beatles gave their first TV performance – he was also a leading thinker who published two books on living in cities. Sadly, the Dome of Discovery can no longer be seen, except in photos. The whole site, apart from Festival Hall, was dismantled in 1952.

Ilmari Tapiovaara

Before IKEA, there was Ilmari Tapiovaara's plywood Domus chair, which he developed with his wife, Annikki, in 1946. This chair, with its distinctive short arms that allowed it to be pulled close to a table, was packaged in a small box and shipped all over the world. It reflected Tapiovaara's focus on producing good design for the many, as did his work with the UN's development program in Paraguay and Mauritius. He produced a number of notable designs that endure, including his Trienna table, which looks like a sharp wooden paw; his simple Kiki range, with upholstered cushions on supporting steel tubes with no arms; and his Pirkka stool, a darker, more traditional stool that was designed for a sauna.

Born in 1914 in Finland, he graduated from the Central School of Applied Arts in 1937, before becoming what many described as Finland's 'second designer' after Alvar Aalto (p.8). He established a studio with Annikki, in 1951 — typically, his name was attached to all of the work that came out of the studio, and her name mainly dropped off, making it hard to say which works were collaborative.

U is for
Untitled

Much of the furniture that Charlotte Perriand designed is labelled 'Untitled', including the bookcase illustrated at right. It seems appropriate; her approach to work was always about function, not form. She didn't see design as art, but rather as a chance to solve problems, to propel people into the future using modern ideas and modern techniques.

Even though her furniture – primarily her collaborations with Le Corbusier (p.52) and Pierre Jeanneret (p.46), including the LC4 chaise lounge – remains famous and her architecture still stands, Perriand has been mostly forgotten. That's partly down to Le Corbusier. He was so much larger than life, so good at branding, that it's easy to see why Perriand's story has been subsumed into his narrative.

Ironically, Le Corbusier didn't initially want Perriand to be part of his story at all. When she approached him for a job in 1927, fresh from a degree in furniture design at the Union centrale des Arts décoratifs, he turned her away, saying, 'We don't embroider cushions here'. It was only once he saw Perriand's *Bar sous le Toit* (Bar in the Attic) display at the Salon d'Automne in the same year, where she displayed a bar full of chrome furniture, that he changed his mind, offering her a job leading his furniture department. Perriand, along with Le Corbusier's cousin and business partner Pierre Jeanneret, did the practical design and prototyping behind Le Corbusier's iconic furniture, including the B301 reclining chair and chaise lounge.

Yet Perriand's story extends so much further than Le Corbusier. While she worked in his studio for ten years, her theories and designs continued to evolve across her productive and extensive career (she designed well into the 1990s). At the beginning of her career, she'd been a passionate advocate for steel; but by the time she designed the Untitled bookcase in the 1950s, she was working with wood. Perriand's materiality became warmer in the 1930s, even more so when she visited Japan as a guest of the Department of Trade Promotion in 1940, and then Vietnam, where she remained until she returned to Paris after World War II ended.

As a designer, Perriand looked to the future; she wanted to help create where we're going, not follow orthodoxy. This is clear in her later work, particularly her kitchen design for Le Corbusier's apartment experiment, Unité d'Habitation in Marseilles. Rather than a wall between the living room and the kitchen, she used a high counter so that the cook – in this time almost guaranteed to be a woman – could remain part of the living space and part of the action.

U is also for

UN Headquarters

The soaring ideals of the United Nations were to be matched by a soaring modernist complex, built on land in New York donated by the Rockefellers. As suited to the collaborative and multi-nation function of this new international body (established after World War II), the winning design of the headquarters was decided by a committee of 13 architects from 13 different countries, including Le Corbusier (p.52) from France and Oscar Niemeyer from Brazil.

The committee selected designs from both Le Corbusier and Niemeyer. It probably comes as no surprise that Le Corbusier acted as the senior architect; Niemeyer reflected later that he was happy to be guided by modernism's leading architect. Whereas Niemeyer had imagined a square in the centre of the UN Headquarters, connecting all the buildings, Le Corbusier insisted on having the Assembly building smack bang in the middle of the compound – it was, after all, the heart of the UN's function. There were six buildings in total; the most dominant is the Secretariat building, a 39-storey structure that holds all of the administrative functions of the UN.

The complex was completed in 1952, three years after the groundbreaking ceremony in 1948. Cost cutting meant the buildings were never big enough for their purpose, and the whole complex was refurbished in 2017.

Utility furniture

There was nothing sexy about Utility furniture. It was, quite simply, utilitarian – and not in an appealingly machinist, Jean Prouvé (p.71) way.

There was a shortage of furniture in Britain during World War II; both materials and talented makers were scarce. But newly married couples still needed furniture, as did people whose homes had been bombed. Enter the Utility Furniture Scheme – a program that produced basic furniture using as few materials as possible, requiring assembly with as little specific skill as possible. Decoration and ornamentation went out the window, by pure necessity. Instead of plywood and metal, the designs used veneered hardwood. At its peak, hundreds of firms in the UK were producing Utility furniture.

After the war and at the end of rationing and coupons, not even the Labour government's enthusiasm could keep the program going – the British public were over it. Nonetheless, the simple, unornamented forms of Utility furniture are now highly sought after as collectors' items.

Jørn Utzon

Louis Kahn (p.50), hardly a schlub in the architecture department, said of Jørn Utzon's Sydney Opera House: 'The sun did not know how beautiful its light was, until it was reflected off this building'. This was no exaggeration – the structure, a vision of white sails perched on an outcrop of Sydney Harbour, is one of the most attractive buildings in the world. The beauty of the building makes it even more devastating that Utzon never got to see his masterpiece complete and shining over the harbour.

Utzon won the competition to design a new opera house for Sydney in 1957; his bold concept was championed by panel member Eero Saarinen. It was Utzon's biggest commission to date, although his list of projects was already diverse. The opera house was going to be big, a massive construction that would demand crazy feats in concrete engineering. But after working on the project for ten years, Utzon resigned under massive pressure due to infighting in Sydney's notorious political scene. The project was completed by local architects. Even though the city council and state government tried to make amends to Utzon, the architect never revisited the city.

Utzon was a true artist, happy working on small or large canvases. Although he has come to be defined by the Sydney Opera House, he completed other remarkable projects that the sun is probably equally as happy to shine on, like his Kuwait National Assembly or his warm, stone holiday retreat, Can Lis on Majorca.

V is for
Von Sternberg House

It was a castle of aluminium and glass in the middle of a semi-rural field, with a moat around the perimeter. Just like a castle, it formed a self-contained world that was a retreat from the busyness of nearby Los Angeles. Von Sternberg House was built in 1935 and was one of the most famous homes designed by Richard Neutra (p.62), a modernist architect who always put the client above a grand idea – unless, of course, the client demanded a grand idea. That's exactly what happened with Von Sternberg House.

Neutra was born in Vienna and immigrated to America in 1923. He first worked with Frank Lloyd Wright, before joining the practice of his friend, housemate and colleague Rudolf Schindler. Neutra established his own office just as the Great Depression hit. Not great timing, but Neutra managed to flourish, taking on private commissions for wealthy clients like Josef Von Sternberg, a director famous for his work with German actress Marlene Dietrich, the woman who intrigued the world.

Von Sternberg House is an idiosyncratic house, specifically designed to suit Von Sternberg's lifestyle. It made a dramatic statement, as a ship floating on a grass sea, with one bedroom and one bathroom inside, a large area for dogs and multiple garages for cars. While there are elements of machine-age modernism on display – like the industrial windows with shading, and the geometric lines of the interior – it's too personal to stick closely to the rules of a particular architectural style.

This is true of Neutra's work in general. He continually experimented and evolved – the house that established his reputation, Lovell House, was the first steel house in America. He also designed four homes for the pioneering Case Study Houses Program (p.16).

Many of Neutra's homes have been demolished, which is surprising, considering he was one of the most famous architects to ever work in Los Angeles. But his homes dot the city; not just large statement houses, but smaller homes, each one personal. Von Sternberg House has also been demolished; it no longer sails through the San Fernando Valley, and only lives on in photos and stories.

V is also for

Villa Planchart

Villa Planchart in the Venezuelan capital of Caracas is designed to be experienced. Its relatively simple facade hides an interior of different angles, perspectives and surfaces, creating a home of light, colour and tactility. You might think that its profusion of personality would be overwhelming – after all, there's a jungle of different coloured marble on the floor, murals on some of the ceilings, yellow stripes on others and plants everywhere – yet it all works. Villa Planchart was designed by Gio Ponti (p.71) for Anala and Armando Planchart, who flew to Milan to interview Ponti. They rejected his initial suggestion of a Spanish-style hacienda; Anala wanted a light and open house, and Armand wanted to fill it with his plants.

The home sits on top of a hill, its exterior a cousin to Le Corbusier's (p.52) Ronchamp chapel, with the roof of the white geometric structure perched like a butterfly. The structure itself – well, Ponti likened it to a modern Florentine villa, one that celebrated artistry and modern materials. He designed for the Plancharts' lifestyle, and this collaboration was a rare meeting of minds. The house is now protected by a foundation, ensuring that it will not be knocked down, remaining as a tribute to imagination, colour and the conviviality of a shared vision.

Arne Vodder

Arne Vodder is most famous for his cabinets. Working with rosewood and teak, he made low sideboards with the wood ingeniously cut to form handles, which he would often paint with bright colours. He was born in Copenhagen in 1926 and trained at the Royal Danish Academy of Fine Arts under Finn Juhl (p.47), who became his mentor and friend; but his work is not as wildly experimental as Juhl's. Like his mentor, Vodder didn't start out dedicating himself to furniture full-time, but opened a studio with Anton Borg in 1951 where they designed affordable homes, as well as furniture.

His cabinets are instantly recognisable (and often copied). As for his chairs, their silhouettes are immediately identifiable as mid-century modern furniture – simple wood frames with plainly upholstered cushions. Vodder's furniture was incredibly popular throughout the '50s and '60s, and often ended up in presidential offices, including the White House when Jimmy Carter was in charge.

Vitra

Vitra, one of the most influential furniture companies in the world, would not exist without Charles and Ray Eames (p.24). Willi and Erika Fehlbaum, who had founded Vitra as a fittings company in Switzerland in 1937, were on a trip to America in 1953 when they saw chairs designed by the Eameses, and fell hard. These chairs weren't being sold in Europe, and neither were any other designs that were being manufactured by Herman Miller, who made and distributed the Eameses' furniture in the US. So the Fehlbaums licensed all the Herman Miller designs, and from 1957 manufactured and sold them in Europe.

But the Fehlbaums didn't stop there. They championed designers' visions, like Verner Panton's out-there plastic, stackable S-chair, illustrated below, which looks like it could fit in with *The Jetsons* decor. They eventually ended their relationship with Herman Miller and set up their own partnerships directly with designers. While Vitra continue to support new design, they are grounded in their history and the history of modern design: purchasing Artek (the company co-founded by the Aaltos, p.8) in 2013 and establishing a design museum that just might have the most comprehensive collection of chairs in the world.

W is for

Wegner

Hans J. Wegner wanted to make the perfect chair. Even though he dabbled with a few other objects, like lights and tables, he was a chair-man through and through. He studied chairs from all different periods, and developed between 500 to 1000 different chair designs over his career (depending on who you ask), of which around a hundred are still in production. That's a lot of chairs.

He was only a few chairs into his career when some people thought he'd already achieved perfection: the Round chair, which the American public came to call 'The Chair', and is still in production today. It's a chair stripped back to the essentials, with a curved back support and a woven or leather seat, the whole thing inspired by Chinese designs from the 18th century. You can't see the joins, courtesy of Wegner's skill as a craftsman. When it was released, *Interiors* magazine in America put it on their cover with the words: 'Is this the most beautiful chair in the world?'

Wegner grew up embedded in the craft movement: his dad was a cobbler, and Wegner was apprenticed to a master cabinetmaker before attending the School of Arts and Crafts in Copenhagen. It's no surprise, then, that he chose to make most of his chairs out of wood; to construct chairs that could be mass-produced yet still acknowledge craft, provenance and nature.

After leaving university, he joined the office of Arne Jacobsen (p.44) — yes, *that* Arne Jacobsen — and Erik Møller, where he was in charge of drawing the furniture for Aarhus City Hall. When this project was completed Wegner set out on his own, establishing his studio in 1943. After all, he had a lot of chairs to design.

It was at this point that he designed the Round chair, closely followed by the Wishbone chair, which became Wegner's most enduring design, as illustrated in the middle on right. While all of Wegner's chairs were designed to be mass-produced — albeit made in Denmark, as Wegner was proud to make Danish chairs — they all needed to be touched by the hand of a talented craftsperson.

He continued to design chairs — from classics to the more playful and snuggly Papa Bear chair, illustrated at bottom right — until he died in 2007.

W is also for

Edward Wormley

American furniture designer Edward Wormley, born in 1907, was one of the six male modernist designers showcased in the iconic 1961 *Playboy* spread that also featured Charles Eames (p.24), George Nelson (p.60) and Jens Risom (p.78), yet his name is now largely forgotten. This is most likely because, even though his designs have a similar aesthetic to the other designers featured in the spread, he did not approach design as egalitarian. His designs were manufactured by Dunbar – where he was head of design for over 30 years – and produced in small quantities, using expensive materials.

The illustration below shows Wormley's Listen-to-me chaise, which looks like it belongs in a design-conscious therapist's office. Its lightweight frame is made of bent laminated wood, designed to give the appearance of floating above the ground; its body undulating tube cushions filled with rubber. Apart from chairs, he also designed carpets, fabrics and lamps.

Peter Womersley

Peter Womersley's first architectural commission was a house for his brother which featured a room known as the Dancefloor: a double-height living room with built-in speakers. It was a glimpse at Womersley's talent for creating delight through design, and also pleasing his clients – particularly his party-loving brother. Yet he was never as prolific as he should have been for the scale, scope and sexiness of his buildings. This is probably because he lived in the Scottish Borders, worked alone and designed most of his buildings in that area.

He was born in 1923, and studied at the Architecture Association in London after serving in World War II. He was attracted to the Scottish Borders after designing possibly his most famous house for textile artist Bernat Klein. Klein House is a naturally warm wood, stone and glass building equalled in charm – in a different way – by Womersley's subsequent studio for Klein, a concrete castle hidden in the verdant landscape near the house. As well as private homes, Womersley also designed public buildings that stand as stark, solid reminders of his talent for constructing geometric shapes using concrete.

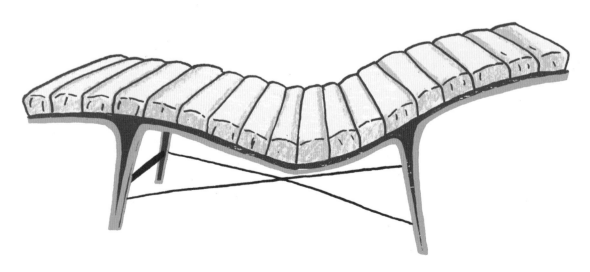

Tapio Wirkkala

Like most Finnish modernist designers, Tapio Wirkkala designed for function, but didn't forget about form. His famous Ultima Thule glassware line looks like dripping icicles, inspired by the freezing temperatures and remote areas of his native Finland. This design only feeds into one of the legends about Wirkkala, which says that while artistic director for iconic Finnish glassware company Iittala (p.42), Wirkkala would retreat to a house in Lapland where no car could reach him – so prototypes had to be flown in by helicopter.

Born in 1915, Wirkkala trained as a sculptor, but is most famous for his work in glass and tableware, as well as the wide array of other objects he designed for the home, like his tables for furniture company Asko Oy with their obvious linear grain, and a lamp for the Aaltos' company, Artek. He set no limitations on himself or on materials; everything was design and everything was open for interpretation. He believed that you should work in harmony with materials, rather than forcing your will upon them. Although he created his most famous work in the 1950s and 1960s, you can see his continuing influence in some glassware lines at IKEA.

Donald Wexler

Donald Wexler was Palm Springs' (p.68) man of steel – an architect who pioneered steel prefab houses, where the frame could be built in a factory. He developed this concept as part of a new housing subdivision for developers George and Robert Alexander, but the rising price of steel meant that only seven of the planned 38 homes were built.

He was one of the architects, along with Albert Frey and E. Stewart Williams, who'd been lured to Palm Springs and then stayed, playing a big hand in its modernist look. In fact, he also designed Palm Springs International Airport.

Although working with steel places him alongside contemporaries like Pierre Koenig (p.51), you only have to look at his Royal Hawaiian Estates in Palm Springs to see that he wasn't a dedicated modernist in the serious Mies van der Rohe sense of the word. Designed with his partner, Richard Harrison, the Royal Hawaiian Estates was an explosion of kitsch, a frenzy of fun. While Wexler can't be blamed for the Hawaiian music that was piped through the complex, he did use bold colours and strong geometric shapes reminiscent of boats to suggest the South Pacific.

E. Stewart Williams

Legend has it that Frank Sinatra walked into the office of Williams, Williams and Williams (the architecture firm set up by E. Stewart Williams' brother and father) in Palm Springs, walked over to E. Stewart Williams and said, 'I wanna house'. What he asked for was a Georgian mansion, which might have melted in the desert sun. Instead, Williams convinced Sinatra to go for a modernist design – a low-slung house with big glass windows and a piano-shaped pool. The only caveat? It had to be built by New Year's Eve, so Sinatra could have a raging party. Williams got it done, and a modernist legend was born.

You might think that he stopped designing at this point – who could top designing Sinatra's house? But Williams was a prominent architect for decades, working around Palm Springs (p.68) and Coachella Valley designing private houses and public buildings.

X is for

X-Chair

While modernist furniture picked up the design world and shook it, this new style didn't come out of nowhere. Each piece has a story, a language, a past. The X-Chair, with its distinctive crossed-over 'X' legs, was inspired by both Ludwig Mies van der Rohe and Lily Reich's Barcelona chair and also by curule chairs from ancient Rome.

The X-Chair was designed by Preben Fabricius and Jørgen Kastholm, who'd opened a studio together in 1961, having met while studying at the School of Interior Design in Copenhagen. Fabricius had a background in cabinet-making and studied under the famous Niels Vodder, who collaborated with Finn Juhl (p.47); and Kastholm had trained as a metalworker and an architect. Even though their furniture is distinctive, they are written in the language that we've come to know as Danish mid-century modern design.

Just like Juhl, Fabricius and Kastholm designed chairs that looked like art – but stripped back, simplified art. Their studio was almost ascetic in their approach to furniture; the pair collaborated on all their designs and only manufactured in small numbers. That is, until they were approached by Alfred Kill, who owned German furniture company Kill International. He wanted to manufacture their furniture – and he was prepared to pay a lot for the privilege. Luckily for us, Fabricius and Kastholm accepted, and they proceeded to create chairs that, while still artistic, could be mass-produced.

At first, you look at Fabricius and Kastholm's chairs as simple and minimalist, just as the pair intended, pure constructions in steel and leather. But then you look closer. The Scimitar chair curves around the base in a way that's almost alien, the Grasshopper lounge leans back as if it's about to spring, and their Tulip chair (different from the one designed by Saarinen) reaches its bulbous and curvy form towards the ceiling. With their chairs, including the X-Chair, the joy is in the detail.

While the pair shut their studio in 1968 over creative differences, many of their designs are still in production, still produced in the same factory – and are extremely collectible.

Y is for

Yanagi

In the annals of design, it is often the flashy who are remembered — Le Corbusier (p.52) for his glamorous Villa Savoye, Christopher Wren for his showstopper St Paul's Cathedral, Yamasaki (p.105) for his tall World Trade Center. But maybe, rather than the glamorous, the showstoppers or the tall, it should be the kettles of the world that are more celebrated; the objects that are a pleasure to use, day in, day out. After all, upon completion, the roof at Villa Savoye leaked. That's something that you couldn't forgive in a kettle.

Sori Yanagi designed a functional kettle that definitely didn't leak. Originally released in 1953, and updated by Yanagi in 1994, this stainless-steel kettle, seen to the right, has an almost flat bottom for optimal heating and a handle that folds up. It won a Good Design Award in 1998, and still sells in its thousands every year, although it's more expensive than an ordinary kettle. That's because it can't be made on a truly industrial scale; 15 different factories in Japan are involved in making its components. Also, it was designed to last a lifetime.

In fact, this kettle has a lot to whistle about. Its pristine stainless-steel exterior is a reflection of Yanagi's approach to design, which was influenced by both modernism and the arts and crafts movement. Yanagi's father, Soetsu, was a leading scholar and proponent of this movement in Japan, and co-founded the Japanese Folk Crafts Museum. Soetsu believed that true beauty came through everyday items that were useful and made by hand; that function itself was beautiful. These ideals imbue Sori Yanagi's work, which touched upon many workaday items, from tongs to the backrests on the walls in subways. But you can also see the influence of modernism in Yanagi's work. Yanagi assisted industrial designer Charlotte Perriand (p.88) when she lived in Tokyo during the early 1940s. She similarly advocated for function over form, for design as a way to solve problems; but also for using machines and modern materials in design.

Yanagi's introduction to modernism and his grounding in the crafts movement resulted in a style that is a unique blend of Japanese and Western influences. Take, for instance, his Butterfly stool, illustrated at far right. This stool has two matching halves of moulded plywood joined together using a metal rod and two screws. It used modern materials and modern techniques, yet is referential of an ancient temple roof. Along with the rest of Yanagi's work, it reflects his belief that beauty came after function, or, more accurately, because of function. His stuff works beautifully, and looks beautiful too.

Y is also for

John Yeon

John Yeon both shaped the environment of the Pacific Northwest in America with his architecture, and protected it with his philanthropy — he purchased a stretch of coastline at Chapman Point (which is now a national park) to save it from development. As part of Yeon's story, it's necessary to mention that he was independently wealthy, which allowed this purchase — although it seems almost churlish to point it out, as it in no way dilutes his impact.

Yeon designed 65 buildings — although only 18 were built — most of them houses, including an experimental plywood house. He was a leading proponent of what is called Pacific Northwest modernism, characterised by its use of unpainted wood, and floorplans and lines that aren't rigidly straight. Watzek House, his first and most famous house, typifies this approach. The exterior was built using unpainted timber, which has softened into a blueish grey over time. The house has a deceptively simple front approach, which opens up out back, its timber-and-glass exterior dominated by a pointed eave, almost like a turret, as seen in the illustration below. It was built for a timber magnate, and the interiors are also heavy with rich, warm wood.

While he liked to call himself a small brushstroke sort of architect, it is his big-picture vision for homes, for timber, for the coast, that defines Yeon's legacy.

Minoru Yamasaki

Most people know Minoru Yamasaki because of the fate of his buildings — he was the architect behind the failed multi-building and multi-storey social housing complex Pruitt-Igoe in St. Louis, which was demolished only two decades after construction; and the World Trade Center in New York, destroyed in a terrorist attack in 2001. But this does Yamasaki a massive disservice, as his architectural footprint was influential and diverse.

Born in 1913 in Seattle, Yamasaki studied architecture in Washington and New York, before moving to Detroit and opening his own firm in 1949.

His buildings were grand, reaching. He mainly designed skyscrapers and government buildings, from the soaring sails of the St. Louis Lambert International Airport to the wine stem–esque 11-storey curved concrete base of Rainier Tower in Seattle. His buildings are large and functional, but they all have decorative embellishments — often Gothic arches — that add soul to the facades, and character to the streets.

Z is for

Zeisel

How often do you think about salt and pepper shakers? Probably not enough, considering the frequency with which we reach for seasoning. But if you owned the mother-and-child salt and pepper shakers, illustrated to the right and designed by Eva Zeisel as part of her Town and Country tableware line in the 1940s, you'd probably think about them a lot more, if only to delight in them. They are fun. They are playful. Their flowing form is abstract, warm and gently reflective of dependent familial relationships. But, most importantly, they are easy to use.

Zeisel was one of the first designers to create wares for a more informal approach to dining, following on from Russel Wright's American Modern (p.11). But rather than Wright's simple and functional tableware that barely nods at the melting forms of Surrealism, Zeisel's tableware were works of serious art (although they weren't serious).

Zeisel designed for use and beauty, a philosophy that evolved over her more than 75-year career. While she's most known for the tableware she produced after she moved to America in 1939, Zeisel first rose to prominence in Europe. Born in Budapest in 1906, Zeisel combined her training in painting at the Royal Academy of Fine Arts with an apprenticeship at the side of a leading ceramicist in the Hungarian folk art scene.

Her life was as interesting as her art: she moved to Berlin at the height of the Weimar Republic, where she was commissioned by a German ceramics company to design tableware in 1928; from there, she moved to Leningrad to work at a pottery factory, before heading to Moscow where she was appointed artistic director of Russia's ceramics and glass industry. While in Moscow, she was arrested on suspicion of trying to assassinate Stalin, and was released after 16 months in prison. She made it to Vienna, only to escape just before the Germans marched into Austria. All this before she'd produced the bulk of her recognised work, her American tableware.

You can't shake the sense, when looking at Zeisel's work, that she amused herself with her wares, that she would have had a secret smirk every time she reached for the pepper. You might smirk too — and really, who can ask for more of a salt and pepper shaker that also works really well?

Z is also for

Marco Zanuso

In the post–World War II era, new materials and new technology were in constant supply. Companies wanted to use these new materials to create new designs – and make more money. Enter Marco Zanuso, whose most famous designs were made of foam and plastic. He was born in Milan in 1916 and studied at the Polytechnic University of Milan, and became one of Italy's leading architects (and city planners, industrial designers, teachers and critics).

He didn't treat new technology or materials with kid gloves. His work has a sense of fun and play. Take the Grillo folding phone, designed with his regular design partner, Richard Sapper, which looks like an armadillo crossed with a mouse; the Doney TV, also designed with Sapper, a bulbous shape that looks like you could bounce it and it would survive; or the Lady chair, as seen in the illustration to the right.

You might think that the most notable aspect about the design of the Lady chair is its shape, which is curvy and comfortable and classy. But it's actually made of foam rubber, and was the culmination of Zanuso's years of experimentation with Pirelli engineers (famous for their tyres), who wanted to make furniture out of the material. The chair won a gold medal at the Milan Triennale in 1951, the same year it was released.

Zanotta

Just like Knoll (p.48) and Herman Miller, Zanotta was formed to bring modern design – or, as founder Aurelio Zanotta liked to call it, 'culture' – to the public *and* to make a profit. From 1954 onwards, Zanotta was synonymous with good Italian design and good Italian designers, like Achille Castiglioni, Carlo Mollino and Marcus Zanuso. The company was crazily creative and experimental – it released the Mezzadro tractor seat stool designed by Castiglioni – and crazily successful, remaining one of the most recognisable Italian furniture companies in the world. Oh, and they were also the first company in the world to produce and sell beanbags.

Timeline

1927   Charlotte Perriand joins Le Corbusier's studio as head of furniture, and collaborates on the LC4 chaise

1928   CIAM (Congrès internationaux d'architecture moderne) founded by architects to agree on principles of modernist design

1929   Richard Neutra designs first steel-framed house in Los Angeles, the pioneering Lovell House

1929   Eileen Gray's masterpiece E-1027 built

1930   Russel Wright releases American Modern tableware

1932   Aino Aalto's Bölgeblick glass released by Iitala; it wins the Gold Medal at Milan Triennale in 1936

1933   Bauhaus, the pioneering German school that inspired modernist aesthetics and values, forced to shut by the Nazis

1933   Alvar and Aino Aalto's 'total work of art' Paimio Sanatorium designed

1933   Alvar Aalto's Stool 60 released

1940   Charles Eames and Eero Saarinen's 'Organic Chair' wins the seating category of Museum of Modern Art's (MoMA) 'Organic Designs in Mass Furnishings' competition

1942   First furniture line released by Knoll, including Jens Risom's iconic webbing chair

1945   John Entenza, editor of *Arts & Architecture* magazine, launches Case Study Houses Program with architects like Charles Eames and Eero Saarinen on board

1946   Eames Office releases the LCM chair, their first moulded plywood seat

1946   Cocktail-hour-ready Kaufmann House, designed by Richard Neutra, built and becomes hallmark of desert modernism

1948   Curvy, caffeinated La Cornuta espresso machine by Gio Ponti released

1949   Eames House, designed by Charles and Ray Eames, built

1949   Called the most perfect chair in the world, Hans J. Wegner's Round chair launched

1949   Anni Albers is the first textile artist to have a solo show at MoMA in New York

1950   Lina Bo Bardi's Glass House, a modernist design floating on the rainforest of Sao Paulo, built

1950 Another glass house – Ludwig Mies van der Rohe's Farnsworth House, finally completed

1950 Rose Seidler House, first Australian commission of soon-to-be-iconic modernist architect Harry Seidler finished

1951 Contour, the most iconic mid-century modern chair in Australia, released by designer Grant Featherston

1951 Antelope chair by Ernest Race used in outdoor spaces of Festival of Britain

1951 Lucienne Day's Calyx fabric features at Festival of Britain and is sold by department store, Heal's

1951 The Lady chair, made of foam produced by a tyre company, invented by Marco Zanuso

1952 The foundation of Chandigarh, the modernist capital city of Punjab in India, laid

1952 The startlingly metal-framed Diamond Chair released by Knoll

1952 A building that represents a sky-high vision, the UN Headquarters by Oscar Niemeyer and Le Corbusier, finished

1953 Sori Yanagi designs what is now seen as the almost-perfect kettle

1954 Robin Day comes up with first chair designed out of polypropylene: the stackable, community-hall-friendly Polyside chair

1957 Jørn Utzon wins competition to design a new opera house for Sydney

1957 Vitra launches as a company selling mid-century modern designs to Europe

1958 The most famous lamp in Denmark, Poul Henningsen's PH 5, released

1960 Perhaps the most famous, but certainly the most photographed, mid-century modern home, Stahl House by Pierre Koenig, finished

1960 The capital city of Brazil, the modernist 'utopia' of Brasília, completed

1960 Arne Jacobsen's SAS Royal Hotel in Copenhagen the world's first 'designer' hotel; he created everything down to the cutlery

1961 Dieter Rams, whose industrial designer leadership at Braun eventually changes the way all the products you use look, joins the company

1962 The question mark lamp of Arco by Achille Castiglione designed

1962 TWA Flight Center, whose modernist design by Eero Saarinen reflected the soaring potential of flight travel, opens

1971 The plastic, curvy, effervescent Panthella lamp by Verner Panton released

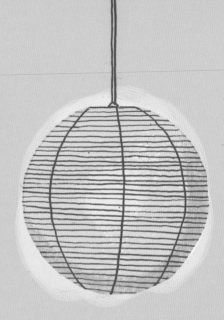

Smith Street Books

Published in 2019 by Smith Street Books
Melbourne | Australia
smithstreetbooks.com

ISBN: 978-1-925811-01-8

All rights reserved. No part of this book may be reproduced or transmitted by any person or entity, in any form or means, electronic or mechanical, including photocopying, recording, scanning or by any storage and retrieval system, without the prior written permission of the publishers and copyright holders.

Copyright text © Lauren Whybrow
Copyright illustrations © Tom Jay
Copyright design © Smith Street Books

The moral rights of the author have been asserted.
CIP data is available from the National Library of Australia.

Publisher: Paul McNally
Project manager: Lauren Whybrow
Editor: Alison Proietto
Proofreader: Isabelle Sinclair
Design concept and layout: Andy Warren
Illustrator: Tom Jay

Printed & bound in China by C&C Offset Printing Co., Ltd.

Book 80
10 9 8 7 6 5 4 3 2 1